IRON SPY

*THE TRUE STORY OF THE GREATEST DOUBLE
AGENT IN WORLD WAR II*

ETHAN QUINN

Polite Note for the Reader's Attention

Anti-Hero has been written in UK English and certain words or phrases might vary from US English. This is except when loyalty to other languages and accents are deemed appropriate.

ISBN- 9781792818783

For Heidi and Nora

CONTENTS

The Life Story Of Eddie Chapman

Aleksandr Solzhenitsyn once said: 'The line dividing good and evil cuts through the heart of every human being.'

Every hero needs a good old-fashioned villain. In fiction, heroes and villains are often depicted as the opposite side of the same coin: Batman and the Joker, Superman and Lex Luthor, Sherlock Holmes and Moriarty. This trope goes on and on and has been a staple of storytelling for centuries.

In some rare cases, however, the two sides of the coin reside within the same person, and no person embodies this more than a forgotten anti-hero by the name of Eddie Chapman.

While it would be unfair to describe Eddie Chapman as an evil man, he certainly had a villainous streak which got him into more than his fair share of trouble.

From a troubled youth all the way up to serving his

country during the Second World War, Eddie Chapman managed to pack more adventure into one life than most people could pack into five.

The story of Agent Zigzag begins in 1942, but Eddie Chapman was so much more than this mere title. He somehow managed to live the life of James Bond before James Bond was even an idea. His travels took him to every dark corner of Europe, and in his wake, he left more than a few broken hearts still yearning for his touch. Of course, Chapman may not have been the direct inspiration for James Bond, but his duplicitous espionage lifestyle would not have looked out of place in any fictional spy thriller story.

Eddie Chapman started out his adult life in the army, but a dishonourable discharge soon led him down the pathway to petty crime—an obvious career choice for anyone with a taste for danger and enough intelligence to outsmart authorities and victims alike. During the Second World War, Chapman worked as a double agent for both the German army *and* MI5, eventually earning himself the moniker of 'Agent Zigzag'. Such a nickname was assigned to Chapman thanks to his less-than-legal extracurricular activities pre-dating the war, showcasing his ability to easily walk the line between good and evil.

When the Second World War ended, Chapman had been once again dispensed of by the war effort and found himself at a loss. This led him to drift back towards a life of petty crime, with his previous good service during the war allowing him to evade any kind of punishment. From this point, his life gradually became stranger and more unfathomable, taking him on some rather unbelievable adventures that even by today's standards, might sound a little exaggerated. The beautiful part, however, is that every incident that follows is as real as the mud on Chapman's boots and the scars on his body.

Eventually, Eddie Chapman was able to turn things around and instil a sense of normality in his life, and in true Zigzag fashion, he managed to craft something of a comfortable existence for himself by the time his final days rolled around.

So, how did the elusive Eddie Chapman manage to fashion such an extravagant life, given his humble beginnings and his foray into an inescapable lifestyle of espionage and danger?

To see how the man forever remembered as Agent Zigzag came to be, it requires a look into his childhood and the events that formed him.

Chapman was a typical product of the harsh North East of England, and this showed throughout his early life into his late teens. In his own words, he later claimed: 'I mixed with all kinds of tricky people', and it was these tricky people who would come to influence the bulk of his life. During his early years, Chapman held many different jobs before finally taking the plunge into a life of crime, with his preferred being fraud and burglary. He gradually rose up through the criminal ranks, with the proceeds from his crimes affording him an extravagant lifestyle filled with expensive clubs and exotic women. It was these two particular crimes—burglary and fraudulent activity—combined with his unrestrained lifestyle that led to him becoming a criminal wanted by the police, eventually resulting in his arrest during his teenage years. While on bail, Chapman fled to Jersey but couldn't resist the allure of the criminal way of life. By the time the Second World War broke out, Chapman was imprisoned in Jersey, missing the first two years of the battle until the German forces eventually occupied Jersey.

It was here that Eddie made a deal with the German forces. He agreed to operate as a German spy, resulting in a search for him by the British government, who wanted Chapman's expertise to work for the Allied side. The German army had paid Chapman a considerable amount to work as an undercover spy for them, but Chapman's love for his country was one of the few things Chapman favoured over money. In addition, he figured if he could work for the British government whilst concurrently being paid by the enemy, he would receive the best of both worlds. He could be a war hero and get rich on the enemy's dime.

He undertook a number of operations, proving himself to

be so skilled in espionage that the German army awarded him a military medal. He ended up with two fiancées, in addition to a harem of women whom he had promised to marry once his war activities ceased. From here, he developed something of an ego complex, rapidly becoming more erratic and difficult to handle. This only proved that MI5 had been right in awarding him the codename Agent Zigzag.

Chapman was then dismissed from MI5 and returned to his previous life of crime. This time, however, he had an ace in his pocket. He used his service throughout the war as a means to get out of trouble whenever he was caught.

He finally gave up his life of crime and moved towards more legitimate means of supporting himself and his family. By this point in his life, he had chosen a wife from the multitude of women he had been stringing along, and had begun a life as a businessman and author.

Chapman's story is one of love, violence, crime, and redemption. It's the story of one man who lied, cheated, and stole his way to one of the most incredible stories to come out of the Second World War. Agent Zigzag had such an impact on the war effort that his life was made into a movie, in addition to numerous documentaries covering his life story. His move into popular culture comes from his achievements during the war, as well as the romanticised views of crime. His intricate skill in the art of seduction adds an element of danger to his life that attracts interest from all quarters. With all this being said, the story of Agent Zigzag isn't one of plain sailing. Eddie Chapman was many things in his life: lover, thief, husband, father, good, bad, but the main thing he will always be remembered as is a spy. You may feel that Eddie Chapman's misdeeds outweigh the good that he did, but there is no denying that despite his evil doings, he still managed to cross over that line between good and evil when necessary.

Chapter 1: Troubled Youth

Edward Arnold Chapman was born on the 16 November 1914, almost four months into the First World War. He was born in Burnopfield, a small village in the North East of England known for its lack of affluence. His father had been a marine engineer before the war broke out but was too old for conscription. This led to him becoming the landlord of a run-down pub named the Clippership in the nearby area of Roker. The joining of his heavy drinking father and a pub wasn't a happy one, as young Eddie was left to his own devices for much of the time. His father doing more drinking than serving meant the family growing up with very little money, often struggling to acquire basic necessities.

Eddie was the oldest of three children in the Chapman household, and the lack of a father figure and lack of money led to Eddie's less-than-dedicated approach to his schooling. This could be partly be attributed to the strain of feeling like a father to his younger siblings, or it simply could have been that Chapman desperately wanted his father to show more of an interest in his daily life.

Eddie's father was significantly more interested in drinking the profits at the Clippership than he was providing any kind of parenting to Eddie and his siblings. This bled through as the Chapman children soon developed a reputation for being troublemakers and tearaways throughout their local area. Eddie, in particular, was a bright child, but the absence of any kind of parenting or guidance gave rise to an unfavourable attitude towards authority. His intelligence was countered by his laziness and inclination to be rude to teachers rather than taking their advice on board. This meant that, despite being perfectly competent to complete and carry out the work that was set for him, Eddie simply preferred to skip school altogether.

In the modern world, Eddie would have been described as a gifted child who was in danger of not reaching his potential. However, early 20th century attitudes towards children meant that Eddie was seen as a disobedient, rude young man. Teachers doled out punishments to him, but he felt they didn't matter because his punishments weren't reinforced when he returned home. As time went on, Eddie decided that it was more convenient not to turn up at school at all. He began to play truant, spending his time at the beach rather than in any of his classes. Strangely, this was where young Eddie Chapman made his first foray into the business world. Here, at the nearby beach, he discovered that plenty of people left lemonade bottles lying around, and he also found that a shop half a mile away redeemed the lemonade bottles for a penny each. Seizing the opportunity to make a little money, Eddie spent his days collecting lemonade bottles then exchanging them for cash. This sudden influx of money, while only a minor amount, led to Eddie Chapman spending much of his time at the local cinema, watching the moving pictures of the day. Quite often, it was Alfred Hitchcock films that took his fancy, foreshadowing the mystery and intrigue that was to follow in the rest of his life.

Eddie often blamed his early life for his later forays into crime. His mother had died of TB when he was very young, his father displayed very little affection or desire to even bring up his children, and there was very little money to spare in the Chapman household. All of these were factors that Eddie chose at will, and sometimes all of them together, to explain why he gravitated towards a life of crime. However, as the next step after playing truant showed, this wasn't exactly the case.

It was Eddie's lack of respect for authority and unwillingness to play by the rules set by society that led to the next big shakeup in his formative years. By the time Eddie was seventeen, he had left school without any qualifications, and his prospects didn't live up to the promise he had shown earlier in his life.

He decided to take on an apprenticeship at an engineering

firm in nearby Sunderland. It wasn't too far from the pub his father ran, and it allowed him the opportunity to progress into a job with a potential future. Unfortunately, like many times before, Eddie soon got bored of working for a living, especially with the apprenticeship being an unpaid position during the initial learning stages.

What other choices were there for a 17-year-old with no qualifications? Eddie didn't really know which avenues to pursue next, so he chose what he felt was the only option available to him. He decided to join the Coldstream Guards.

Being just 17 meant that Eddie needed to lie about his age to receive access, but this was a common occurrence at the time. It didn't take much convincing for the tall and charismatic Chapman to talk his way to acceptance. It was because of this set of circumstances that led to Eddie Chapman joining the Second Battalion of the Coldstream Guards and becoming their youngest member.

By this point, the First World War had ended, so Eddie didn't see any service time, but he was still made to endure the basic training. It was harder work than the young Chapman expected, but he still threw himself into it with aplomb. So much, in fact, that while playing handball as a training exercise he fell and sliced his knee open. It was a severe wound that required stitches and left an obvious and unpleasant looking scar, and it would be this scar that authorities would use as an identifying feature years later.

Once Eddie had finished his basic training, he was placed on sentry duty outside the Tower of London. While this position held prestige, Eddie Chapman, in typical fashion, found his new role somewhat boring and embarrassing. His bright red uniform combined with the tall bearskin hat meant that he stood out in the busy city, causing people to stare and, in many cases, laugh at him. For someone who saw himself as something of a Casanova, Eddie found this minor humiliation difficult to bear. This feeling of boredom inspired Eddie's innate sense of adventure to come bubbling to the surface.

Despite his reluctance, this position became Eddie's most stable and legitimate job, one he lasted in for nine months. He would never again manage such a tenure at anything legitimate without dipping his toes into the pool of criminality.

At the nine-month point, Eddie was allowed to take six days' leave. He informed the sergeant major that he was taking a trip back to the North East to see his father, to which the sergeant major consented. Eddie had been in London for a significant time at this point and by now had come to miss his family.

During his time at the Tower, Eddie had come under the influence of a more experienced guardsman. While it would be unfair to call him a bad influence, as Eddie hardly needed any encouragement, the more experienced colleague of Eddie's took him on a whistle-stop tour of some of the less-than-wholesome places around the West End of London and Soho. Eddie spent what free time he had drinking and dancing in the clubs and cafes of Soho, eyeing up each beautiful woman as though he were an untamed animal on the loose.

During his late-night excursions, one girl in particular caught his eye. Eddie didn't know it yet, but she would to be the beginning of a lot of his trouble.

The girl was a stunning brunette—young, slim, and as adventurous as Chapman himself. While it was true that she laid eyes on him first, once he spotted her, he couldn't quite avert his gaze. That same night, Eddie stayed at hers, and it would be the first time he ever made love to a woman.

Perhaps it was the thrill of a first love, perhaps it was because it was his first time, but she managed to persuade Eddie to stay one more night. Before he knew it, another night turned into two months, and during this, they had managed to burn through all Eddie's small salary.

It was once Eddie's pay had been used up that the police came searching for him. Naturally, this gave Eddie suspicions about the new lady in his life. Was it possible she had tipped off the police regarding Chapman's absenteeism from the forces once his money had run out?

It was something he never found out for sure, but he always held the belief that she had.

Eddie was arrested on the charge of going absent without leave. Luckily, this meant that he wouldn't spend time in a regular prison, instead being condemned to a military prison. His sentence was eighty-four days in the military compound at Aldershot.

During this time, his primary job was to scrub out bed pans, something Eddie believed was an unduly harsh punishment. Although Eddie served his time without causing too much drama, this initial imprisonment served only to ramp up his distaste for authority. When his eighty-four days were up, he left the prison with a bad taste in his mouth. It didn't matter to him that he had brought the prison stint upon himself, and it certainly wouldn't be the last time a woman was the reason why he willingly undertook something so foolish.

All Eddie had left after his prison stint was his suit and £3 in his pocket.

While £3 may not sound like much, it would be worth around £190 today. It wasn't enough to buy a house, but it was enough to keep him sustained while he reintegrated himself into the outside world.

Eddie fully intended to get himself back on his feet, but he didn't intend to play by the rules that the establishment had set for him. With everything he owned on his back, he caught a bus into London and planned his next step.

In a stroke of luck almost bordering a miracle, Eddie Chapman managed to land himself a job as a barman quite soon following his release from prison. It wasn't what he wanted to do, but it was preferable to starving. The hours were decent, and it meant he could get to know some of the criminal element of Soho. Despite this, he didn't stick at it for too long. Instead, he used the opportunity to progress to other jobs: a masseur (which almost persuaded him to go straight back to the bar work), a film extra, a boxer, a wrestler, and even a dancer—all ended up on Eddie's CV.

In a strange twist of fate, it was his short-lived job as a wrestler that started his connection to the criminal underworld. Pimps and confidence tricksters were just some of the people he created a rapport with, which in turn gave him links with other avenues.

He took to the criminal world like a duck to water. He made good money as a wrestler, but it wasn't good enough to support the lifestyle that Eddie was growing accustomed to. Namely, he had begun to develop an affection for cognac and gambling—two favourite pastimes of the high-end criminal class.

Eddie realised that he must find a way to supplement his income from wrestling if he wanted to join the ranks of the elite. Therefore, he resorted to the aforementioned fraud and petty crime. He would forge cheques or sometimes even straight-up steal them. He began breaking into houses, taking anything that he could fence for significant cash. Eddie's crimes weren't violent or grand in scale, but he still didn't give a second thought to whom he hurt or what he stole. However, such endeavours couldn't last. Despite his mild success, Eddie was impulsive and inexperienced when it came to criminal activity. Sooner or later, he would make a mistake.

1935 wasn't even a month old before Eddie was finally caught in a mistake. That January, he was caught in the back garden of someone's property. While he hadn't broken in, his intentions were plainly obvious. Despite this, the presiding judge was lenient, and Chapman was only fined £10.

The judge's leniency was wasted. In February of the same year, Eddie was caught committing cheque theft and credit fraud. The judge didn't give him the benefit of the doubt this time around, and Eddie's second prison sentence was set at two months. He was placed in Wormwood Scrubs, being tasked with hard labour amongst the general prison population.

His time inside Wormwood Scrubs came to no effect, as it certainly didn't teach Eddie much of a lesson. Three weeks following his release, he was locked up again with a change of scenery, being sentenced to three months inside Wandsworth Prison for trespassing and attempted housebreaking.

Eddie Chapman found himself on a downward spiral, and it didn't take long for him to be in trouble with the law again. This time, however, it wasn't petty theft. In the early weeks of 1936, he was found guilty of 'behaving in a manner likely to offend the public'. It wasn't revealed exactly what Eddie had done to carry out his wholesale offence of the general public, but there were plenty of rumours flying around.

By this time, Eddie had fully immersed himself in the life of a petty criminal. He wasn't only carrying out low level crimes, he was also cavorting with sex workers in his spare time. The main rumour about Eddie at this time was that he had been caught in public engaging in a carnal act with a prostitute. Eddie once again found leniency from the court and was just fined £4 and ordered to pay the doctor who had tested him for sexually transmitted diseases. Once more, it only took two weeks for Eddie to be caught committing petty crimes again. This time, he was arrested for fraud after he tried unsuccessfully to avoid a bill at a hotel. Eddie was fast becoming a career criminal, and the rate at which he was getting caught also meant that he wasn't a particularly good one.

His life revolved around evenings spent in a lavish manner of some sort. He enjoyed being seen at the clubs in Soho, usually romancing beautiful women. Of course, sometimes his advances were simply a ruse, as his criminal mind now realised he could extort money from those he slept with. After all, Eddie was a handsome man, and women found him incredibly charming. He used these skills to seduce married women and, with the aid of a partner, blackmailed these women when he presented them with photographs of their adultery.

However, Eddie was treading on thin ice, as his crimes didn't pay well enough to allow him a break, and he also wasn't a smart enough criminal to carry out his transgressions without leaving some trace of evidence. It was only a matter of time before Eddie would begin to spend more of his time in jail than out of it.

Oddly, he'd even begun to indulge in some prostitution himself to help make ends meet. When it came to funding his lifestyle, it was clear that there was nothing Eddie wouldn't do. However, things soon started to change when Eddie met a gentleman named Jimmy Hunt.

It was during one of Eddie's many stints in jail that Eddie met Jimmy. Jimmy was, in many ways, the polar opposite of Eddie. He was cool and collected, methodical and driven. Most of all, though, he was adept in the ways of the criminal. Jimmy spotted something in Eddie, though, something that led to them working together in a gang, which would shape the trajectory of Eddie's life for the next ten years.

Chapter 2: Making A Name

Jimmy Hunt was known to all as the best safe cracker in the whole of London. It wasn't an idle boast, either. Jimmy had perfected a technique using the newly discovered, to criminals at least, gelignite.

Gelignite is an explosive that is relatively stable, burns slowly, and won't explode without a catalyst to trigger detonation. This made it perfect for use within quarries, but it also made it perfect for breaking into safes. Jimmy Hunt used a technique that was somewhat revolutionary. He would fill a condom with gelignite and water, drill a hole into the lock of the safe, insert the condom into the hole, and then detonate the condom. Due to the condom not being porous but also being pliable enough to be forced into a drilled hole, it was a perfect technique.

In the late 1930s, Jimmy and Eddie recruited two additional members and formed a 'gang' to carry out heists. The first: Antony Latt, an experienced burglar with nerves of steel. The second: Hugh Anson, an accomplished getaway driver, and someone who would eventually have an impact on Eddie's life beyond his criminal activities. Together, they called themselves 'The Jelly Gang' after the gelignite they made regular use of.

Their first heist took place at a fur store called Isobel's, in Yorkshire. They decided on a store reasonably far away from where they lived, on account of their growing reputation throughout London. A job done in another city would be far less likely to be pinned on them. For the first time in his life, Eddie suffered from cold feet. He remained in the car while Latt and Hunt broke into the store and stole a selection of furs and £200. By the next job, Eddie managed to overcome his cold feet, and once again they made the move away from London and targeted a pawnbroker's in Grimsby.

This heist, however, was a much more complex operation. Anson was tasked with creating a diversion of the workers inside, which he achieved by loudly revving the engine of their getaway vehicle. Eddie then used his skills as a petty criminal to break into an empty house next door to the pawnbroker's along with Jimmy. Once inside, they cut through the joining wall between the two buildings and made their way through. While the noise of Anson's car helped to mask this, it wasn't breaking through the wall that caused the real noise. The pawnbroker's contained four safes, each of which Hunt would need to crack using gelignite. The engine revving from outside drowned out the explosions perfectly. Eddie and Jimmy returned to their car with £15,000 worth of goods and cash.

From this point, no longer was Eddie Chapman a petty thief, living on the scraps he could grab from breaking into people's houses. He had arrived on the big stage. The Jelly Gang then went from success to success, even going so far as to carry out jobs in their native London.

During one such job, Hugh Anson somehow managed to wrap their vehicle around a lamppost during a particularly frantic escape. As commonly happens at the scene of an accident, a crowd formed. One spectator in the crowd laid his hand on the bonnet of the wrecked car. This was a mistake he would live to regret.

The man in question was a small-time thief, not unlike Eddie Chapman before the Jelly Gang. The man's fingerprints were matched up to the Scotland Yard database, resulting in a four-year jail sentence for his crime of being nosey at the scene of an accident.

Eddie Chapman had no trouble spending money before he had become a successful crook. Now he was successful, he began to spend the money almost as quickly as he got it. Just as the Kray twins would 30 years later, Eddie began rubbing elbows with celebrities. He would carry out high paying heists with the Jelly Gang and then spend the proceeds in the places to be seen around London. He was mixing with actors, journalists, authors, and of course, other notorious criminals. His dress sense changed as he began wearing expensive suits from Savile Row. He even spent big on one or two luxury vehicles.

Eddie made no secret of his wealth or how he had achieved it. Everyone knew that Eddie Chapman was a crook through and through. By 1935, the Jelly Gang had become so successful that they had enough money to take a break. The police were nowhere near catching them, instead suspecting an American group to be responsible for the Jelly Gang's recent crimes. This was due to the Jelly Gang's use of chewing gum as an adhesive for the gelignite and the presence of chewing gum at the crime scenes.

Following their surprise success, Eddie and Latt decided they deserved a holiday. They rented a house in Dorset and retired there to relax and to let the heat on them in London die down. Although the police were well off-course with who had carried out the Jelly Gang's crimes, the fact they were looking into their crimes at all meant they needed to be wary.

It only took six weeks for the two men to become bored with their time away. They planned their next heist on a shop in Edgware Road. Eddie disguised himself as an inspector for the local water board and made his way into the house next door to the shop. Once inside the house, Eddie smashed a hole in the joining wall, employing the same *modus operandi* as in the pawnbroker's job. They then removed the shop's safe and took it out to their getaway vehicle, which was then driven to Jimmy Hunt's garage. It was here that Jimmy broke into the safe.

By now, the Jelly Gang were a well-oiled machine, but their confidence resulted in carelessness. Scotland Yard had long since moved on from their chewing gum theory, and the big-spending Eddie Chapman associates were now attracting their attention. It was an inevitable conclusion for the authorities—after all, what other assumption is there when men with no jobs purchase expensive cars and suits on a regular basis? While the Jelly Gang may have left no evidence at their crime scenes, they were most certainly leaving evidence in their personal lives.

By 1937, Scotland Yard had deduced the existence of this mysterious 'gelignite squad', and their sole focus became determining who exactly was a part of their operation. It didn't take long for them to have their crosshairs trained on Eddie Chapman. During 1938, Chapman, Hunt's, and Latt's mugshots were printed in multiple police periodicals. While this wasn't related to the overt spending and conspicuous personal lives, they were suspects in the huge number of recent cinema safe cracks. The Jelly Gang were initially successful because they carried out jobs far away from London, but out of greed and confidence they had started to do jobs closer to home, a risky venture that brought them to the brink of discovery.

By early 1939, the Jelly Gang had realised that the police were aware of their existence and decided to revert to their original *modus operandi*. They loaded up their car with gelignite and made the long trip to Scotland for their next heist. Ironically, it would be their decision to change back to their original, safer method of choosing targets that would lead to their capture and the subsequent break-up of the Jelly Gang.

After the long 12-hour drive, they settled into their high-class hotel on the outskirts of Edinburgh. Their successful crime careers meant that they had got a taste for the high life and had no intention of giving it up now. The gang spent some time at the hotel planning their next move. The choice was a simple one: the Edinburgh Co-Operative Society. It was obvious that there would be a large amount of money kept in their safe, meaning that the trip would be lucrative while putting them out of the reach of Scotland Yard.

The job went off without incident. The gang managed to carry it out quickly and efficiently, with Jimmy Hunt cracking the safe with his usual expertise. While the gang made their way out of the building, Eddie accidentally smashed part of the skylight that he was climbing through. Unfortunately for the group, luck wasn't in their favour this night. Outside, a policeman was making his rounds. At the sound of breaking glass, he blew his whistle to alert other officers in the area.

They had been discovered, albeit completely by chance.

The four crooks made a break for it over a nearby wall. However, Anthony Latt, being of large stature, slipped on the railway tracks that led away from the Co-Operative building. Showing no concern for their fallen comrade, the Jelly Gang left him on the tracks with a broken ankle. They made it to their getaway car and sped away from the scene of the crime in a haze of smoke and screeching wheels. However, it was all to no avail, as they were intercepted by a police car while they made their way south.

The four men were placed in jail in Edinburgh, but in a startling display of incompetence by the Scottish police, the group were immediately granted fourteen days' bail. By the time their case came to court, the men had, unsurprisingly, vanished. Their descriptions were distributed to every police force in the country. The Jelly Gang were no longer under scrutiny; they were wanted men. Their infamy didn't stop them from carrying out further heist jobs up and down the country.

The Jelly Gang made their way to Bournemouth and cracked a safe located inside a Co-Operative store. Latt, now recovered from his injury, made the mistake of writing to his girlfriend to inform her of the Jelly Gang's plans to fly to Jersey and then to the South of France. The letter was intercepted by the police, who now knew the gang's whereabouts and intentions.

Eddie Chapman had convinced the other members to make a detour on their trek to Jersey to pick up his girlfriend, Betty Farmer. In a truly theatrical manner, Eddie arrived at her door and told her she needed to pack her things right away because they were headed for distant shores. Excited at the prospect of a trip to Jersey and France, Betty showed no hesitation. However, Betty was blissfully unaware of Eddie's criminal lifestyle. He had told her he worked in the film industry. It was a convenient way to explain both his money and the time he spent working at odd hours.

Betty was a little taken aback when she got back to the car to find they weren't alone, but she simply accepted the other members of the Jelly Gang as Eddie's colleagues in the film business. Feeling somewhat exhilarated, the group headed to Croydon Airport to catch their flight to Jersey. They caught their plane, and several hours later were checking into the Hotel de la Plage in Jersey, far away from the prying eyes of Scotland Yard.

Less than ten years old, the Hotel de la Plage was a modern hotel that provided the level of luxury that Eddie had become accustomed to. They spent the evening at a local nightclub and casino. It was business as usual for Eddie, but for Betty, it was a step outside of her usual world. She hadn't been taken into Eddie's circle to a great extent before, and the evening of dancing and gambling made her feel like she was a film star. They retired to bed that night with Betty on top of the world. She had no idea what the next day had in store for her.

The following day was a Sunday, and Eddie and Betty planned on resting. It was a beautiful day outside, looking into the sea was like gazing into crystal, and the sun beamed without hindrance. Eddie and Betty made their way to the restaurant of the Hotel de la Plage and ordered their midday meal. It was all-round perfect, but it just whet their appetite for more. They decided to order trifles, and Eddie sat entertaining his belle while they waited. The trifles arrived and were placed in front of them. As they ate, Eddie noticed two men had entered the restaurant, and something about them raised his suspicions. They were wearing overcoats and hats – not exactly holiday appropriate attire.

Eddie's first thought was that they couldn't be guests of the hotel, and he then spotted them having an animated conversation with the head waiter. It was then that Eddie's instincts kicked in, and he realised they were there for him. Eddie stood up, gave Betty a solitary kiss, and launched himself out of the window of the Hotel de la Plage without looking back, causing a scene inside like something out of a Laurel and Hardy act. Plates were smashed, women screamed hysterically, and the two men in overcoats looked at each other, dumbfounded. They rushed to the space where Eddie had thrown himself to see him hurrying off into the distance, beach sand trailing his every step. The two gentlemen climbed out of the window with significantly more grace than Eddie had managed and then took off after him regardless of his head-start. Due to Eddie's athletic prowess, the gap between him and his chasers only widened. The two men gave up their chase, but Eddie kept running. He ran for a mile down the beach and then doubled back. He kept away from main roads in favour of side streets. He found a school that was empty of pupils and staff due to the weekend, so he broke inside to hide.

He found a coat that had been left in the school over the weekend, and as dusk began to fall, he made his way back into town. He discovered a small boarding house just outside the town centre and checked himself in.

The landlady of the boarding house, Mrs Corfield, was wary of travellers entering her establishment and therefore demanded payment in advance. Eddie gave her the small amount of cash he had on him and promised he would pay her the remaining amount in the morning.

He made his way to his room and used a dull penknife to shave off his moustache. Despite the landlady having already seen him, he felt it best to remove as many distinguishing features as possible. He knew that by now there would be people looking for him and that by the morning the newspaper would be full of reports of his escape. With reports would come descriptions, which meant that removing his moustache was the least he could do to try and evade capture.

As darkness fell on Havre-le-Pas, Eddie made his way to

the nightclub where he and Betty had spent the previous evening. Inside was completely empty. He decided to break in and take the money that he needed to pay for his boarding house. Once inside the nightclub, he located the safe, and without the aid of gelignite, broke inside and extracted all the deposited cash—more than enough to pay back Mrs Corfield. He returned to the boarding house and lay down to sleep.

What Eddie didn't know was that while he had been at the nightclub, Mrs Corfield had made a journey of her own. As soon as he had left her house, she pulled on her coat and made her way to the police station. Eddie's escape from the Hotel de la Plage had actually been broadcast on the radio, and almost everyone within a ten-mile radius had become aware of Chapman's notoriety. The moment Eddie had walked through the door of Mrs Corfield's house, she had been aware of his identity. While he was at the nightclub, she had informed the police about the suspicious man currently staying in her house. Eddie's sleep wasn't to last long, and neither was his freedom.

By the time Eddie was arrested, Betty had been in limbo for over 12 hours. She had been questioned repeatedly by detectives, searched by the manager of the Hotel de la Plage, and was becoming incredibly frustrated and upset. She'd been forced to move into a smaller hotel as she had little money of her own, and the Hotel de la Plage was unwilling to keep her on as a guest.

Eddie was captured very quickly following the arrival of officers to Mrs Corfield's boarding house. Knowing that attempt to escape was futile, he gave himself over without resistance. Three weeks later, Eddie Chapman appeared before judge and jury. The first thing Eddie did when he appeared in court was make it clear that Betty had been both unaware of and not a part of the Jelly Gang's heists. The judge informed Eddie that the people of Jersey not only had no quarrel with Betty, but that they also didn't want her on the island anymore. As Eddie was led out of the court, Betty passed a note to him, in what could have possibly been their final communication. It was a long time before Eddie would see Betty again, but he never forgot her.

Eddie's burglarising of the nightclub was a double-edged sword regarding decision-making. If Eddie had not robbed the nightclub, then he would have been extradited back to England to serve the same sentence that Hunt and Latt were now serving, having also been uncovered during their Jersey trek. However, because Eddie committed a crime on Jersey soil, he was obliged to serve a prison sentence for that crime before he was extradited. He pleaded guilty to the crimes of housebreaking and larceny, resulting in a sentence of two years of hard labour in a Jersey jail. His ability at breaking into the nightclub showed the judge that he was both a skilled criminal and had no intention of finding an honest living while on foreign soil. The sentence wasn't ideal for Eddie, but he knew that it was better than the alternative of returning to the mainland.

Eddie soon found out that life in a Jersey jail wasn't the improvement he'd expected. His hard labour was stuffing mattresses for eight hours a day, the irony not being lost as he slept each night on wooden planks with no padding whatsoever. He didn't find his time in the Jersey jail particularly hard, only boring and monotonous. He set about using his charm in an attempt to alleviate some of the boredom.

The governor of the prison was an ex-military gentleman with an affinity for anyone who shared his military backstory. Eddie used this to his advantage by exaggerating his own military experience, which got him a much more interesting and respectable position working in the governor's private garden. Another task of his was to clean the house, which gave Eddie access to all the governor's personal living space.

After four months inside the Jersey jail, Eddie spotted his chance. The governor and his family were going out for the day. Eddie knew he didn't have a moment to lose, so as soon as the governor's car had left the grounds, he put his plan into action. He ceased his cleaning duties and ran upstairs to the governor's son's bedroom. Once there, he went through his wardrobe and found himself an outfit to aid in his escape. Additionally, he liberated a suitcase and filled it with a torch, a poker, a jar of sixpences, and a pair of spectacles. Once he had filled the suitcase, he set about filling his pockets with as much money as he could.

Eddie's plan was a simple one. The Jersey jail wasn't particularly tight on security, a fact he planned to exploit. The governor's house backed onto the prison hospital, so Eddie decided this would be his escape route. He climbed onto the roof of the house and dropped over the wall into the grounds of the hospital. Once inside the hospital grounds, it was a simple case of scaling another wall until freedom was within his grasp.

It took an hour for any of the guards to realise that Eddie Chapman had gone missing. The first time it became apparent was when a guard made his way into the kitchen in the governor's house to check on their captive. He saw the kitchen was empty and uncleaned, so he strolled around the rest of the property, expecting to find Chapman working away in one of the rooms. Alternatively, he also thought perhaps the jovial and charming Chapman was perhaps hiding around the prison grounds as a way to break the monotony of the day.

When the guard still couldn't find him, he enlisted the help of the other guards to help as their minor problem escalated into desperation. With a thorough search by the on-site guards, Chapman was still nowhere to be found. A full two hours after Eddie had made his escape, a search party made up of law enforcement and every guard in the vicinity was assembled. All hotels and boarding houses were both warned and searched, all outbound trains were cancelled, and the roads were crammed with police searching for the missing suspect. In just three hours, Eddie Chapman had turned the sleepy island of Jersey into a panic zone.

Unfortunately, Eddie hadn't fully thought his plan through. He knew exactly how he was going to get out of the jail, but he wasn't as sure about where he could hide on the island. It was a small place where most people were familiar with each other, and he knew it wouldn't take long for his face to be burned into the mind's eye of most of the populace. He knew that he couldn't afford to be seen walking around for long, so he needed another form of transport.

Fortunately for Eddie, a man passing by had offered him a lift, someone who evidently hadn't heard about the escaped prisoner yet. He dropped Eddie at a telephone box, where he phoned the airport. Upon finding out that the last plane for the day had already left, he checked into a hotel and ordered a taxi. Eddie was extremely lucky at this point, as he managed to leave the hotel before any searches reached him. In the back of his taxi, he silently surveyed the island, looking for any method that would afford him escape.

Eventually, he found his answer in a quarry.

Here, he knew that he would be able to source gelignite, which he could then use to earn money, allowing him to then buy a plane ticket and be France-bound within weeks. During the late afternoon, after all the workers had left, Eddie returned to the quarry and, using his considerable skill as a burglar, emerged with an arsenal of explosives and detonators. From here, he didn't know exactly where to go. He couldn't break into anywhere without a way of escaping quickly, which he certainly couldn't do on foot.

In another stroke of luck, he spotted a car that had been left by the side of the road, probably left by lovers who had gone off to find a more private spot, a practice that Eddie was very familiar with. He managed to manipulate the lock and quickly gain access to the stranded vehicle. He threw his hat and some gelignite onto the passenger seat and set about opening the bonnet so he could get the engine started.

Eddie's luck ran out, however, as the owner of the car came back before he managed to get it running. A scuffle soon ensued, although Eddie's athletic ability and strength were too much for his youthful opponent to best. With little effort, Eddie threw the car's owner over a wall, possibly leaving him for dead. Eddie fled, leaving his hat and gelignite behind on the passenger seat. This was not the ending that Eddie had anticipated. To finish off his eventful evening, he found an empty house, broke in, and promptly fell asleep.

The next morning, Eddie had breakfast at a local cafe while pondering his next move. He decided that a boat off the island was his best chance, and he would need some way of acquiring one. He managed to steal some overalls and a shrimping net and made his way to the docks. Eddie looked for a boat that would accommodate him as well as being able to sail him to his destination. The beach he arrived at was crowded, so he didn't notice the two men approaching him from the side. The owner of the cafe had tipped off the police that a man who looked like the escaped prisoner had eaten there in the morning.

Chapman, however, refused to go back to jail without a fight. When the two men approached him and made their intentions known, Chapman instigated nothing short of a riot on the beach, although he was soon overpowered by the two large gentlemen. Accepting defeat, Eddie then agreed to come quietly, mainly because he still had the remaining gelignite in his pockets, and he didn't want anything to cause it to explode.

He was taken back to jail and formally charged with a variety of offences. His jail term was increased by another year when he appeared in court in September. While this was obviously a big deal to Eddie, it was only a small worry to the inhabitants of the rest of the world at the time, as the war between England and Germany had just begun.

Chapter 3: Redemption

Eddie spent a lot of time in jail attempting to improve his education. He'd never had much trouble with learning when he was at school—he'd just found it too boring to give his full attention.

Now that he had only four walls to stare at day after day, he had discovered what true boredom felt like.

This monotony led him to the prison library, where he spent time improving his language skills, French and German in particular. He craved information from the outside world, but useful information was scarce. The war had made people concerned about the information they gave out. People believed that German spies were hiding in every corner of the world, even nestled inside Jersey jails. Any information he did acquire was either unreliable at best, or heart-breaking at worst.

In mid-1940, Eddie received a letter from a dancer that he had been living with during his time in London, a woman named Freda Stevenson.

Freda gave Eddie the somewhat unnerving news that he was a father to a one-year-old daughter. Her surprise letter informed him exactly how bad things had got for her during wartime. Rationing and the closing of most of London's nightlife had left her almost destitute. The purpose of her letter, however, was not just to inform, but to request aid. Freda's letter ended with pleas for money to help her feed his little girl, a request which Eddie was willing to oblige.

However, the governor refused Eddie's request to reply to her letters. Perhaps it was because of Eddie's escape attempt making him and his prison look incompetent in performing their roles, or perhaps it was because the war was also taking its toll on the governor. Regardless of the reason, the refusal had a detrimental effect on Eddie's mental health, sending him spiralling into a pit of despair. What had originally been a stroke of luck was rapidly turning into a very bleak outcome.

June 1940 brought about a pivotal moment in Eddie Chapman's life. Jersey became occupied by the Germans, and there were almost no troops on the island when the Luftwaffe landed. The occupants offered no resistance, and in a short time, Jersey became a territory of Nazi Germany. At first, this meant very little to Eddie—he was in prison and, under German rule, he remained there. As time passed, the effects of the German invasion began to show. Conditions worsened, and food became more and more scarce. Islanders were barely being given enough to eat, and prisoners were given even less. Eddie was already a slender man, but the combination of hard labour in prison and very little to eat reduced him to something of a skeletal figure.

Very soon, the German forces had started to run the island under their own rules. This meant that several new laws had come into effect as well as German-run courts taking session. The meagre food ration in the prison was decreased further by the influx of new prisoners, and Eddie continued to get thinner and thinner.

In December 1940, Eddie Chapman received a new cellmate, a fellow named Anthony Faramus. Faramus, a middle-aged Jersey resident, had been imprisoned for both fraud and carrying anti-German propaganda on his person.

The two, bonding over their criminal origins, became friends almost right away. Faramus was released several months before Eddie, but when Eddie Chapman was awarded freedom in October 1941, he found Faramus waiting outside the prison for him. Since Faramus had been a hairdresser before the war, the two men opened a barber shop upon Eddie's release.

With the main regulars to the barber shop being German officers, it wasn't long before Eddie's criminal ability reared its head. A British man, one of the few who regularly used the services of the barber shop, also happened to be a black-market trader. He bought various illicit and hard-to-get substances from German soldiers and then sold them on to the indigenous citizens of Jersey—for a large profit, of course. Very soon, Eddie's barber shop became the legal front of the Jersey black market. It was the perfect location. German soldiers had no intention of reprimanding them because, for them, it doubled as their regular grooming salon.

By the early 1940s, Eddie Chapman had managed to craft a comfortable yet unusual life for himself. He continued this life of mild deceit, his actions bordering on criminality just enough to appease his compulsion for adventure. Jersey soon became a German stronghold, with Hitler intending to use it as a holiday camp after the war. However, while the war raged on, Jersey served as a strategic base, with huge numbers of German soldiers drafted to stay on the island. In typical Eddie fashion, things couldn't last. He forgot that the Germans had changed the laws of Jersey to suit their own. Included in this: driving on the right-hand side of the road.

One brisk morning in 1941, Eddie set off on the left-hand side of the road on his bike and careered directly into a German officer riding a motorbike. This resulted in Eddie being taken to the police station for interrogation by German officials. He took away a faint and a deeply unsettling feeling that his criminal history may come back to haunt him. This then led to Eddie devising a plan.

He spoke with Faramus when he returned to the barber shop, proposing the idea—fuelled by his genuine disdain with the British government—of offering his services to the Germans as a spy, as a way to get himself sent over to England. Once there, he could escape the German rule of Jersey and use the distraction of the war to get away with his previous crimes. Faramus was wary of the plan, but lacking better alternatives, he tentatively agreed to be a part of it. Together they wrote a letter to be sent to the German command post, then waited on tenterhooks for any kind of response. Less than a week later, they were granted an audience with a German major.

Eddie launched into his best anti-establishment diatribe in an attempt to strengthen his case, but the major only looked back at him with an expression devoid of any kind of emotion. It was obvious that nothing would come from their efforts. They were led out of the Mayor's quarters and returned to the barber shop.

As the old saying goes, no news is good news, but in Eddie and Anthony's case, this couldn't be further from the truth. They heard nothing from the German forces, and so went about their business as they had done before. Both assumed that their request had been rejected. Perhaps they had come across as too keen, revealing themselves to be soldiers too focused on revenge rather than honourable combatants of war. Alternatively, it could have been that Eddie's previous crimes worked against them. Regardless, the two men returned to their life of cutting hair and trading black market goods.

Things changed in December of the same year when Eddie and Faramus were woken one morning by an incessant banging on their front door. When Eddie opened up, still sleepy-eyed and delirious, he was greeted by the Gestapo. Eddie assumed it was all part of an act to make it appear less suspicious when they began their espionage careers. He couldn't have been more wrong. There had been some telephone wires cut across the island, and the remaining Jersey police had claimed that the culprits were Chapman and Faramus. While they weren't guilty of the crime, that was irrelevant to the Gestapo. Eddie and Faramus were arrested and promptly transferred to the Fort de Romainville in Paris for their alleged crimes.

Fort de Romainville wasn't a prison, as such—it was a German concentration camp. On the first day there, Eddie learned from another prisoner that sixteen people had been executed that very morning. It was different from every prison that Eddie had ever experienced. The punishments consisted of beatings, regular and brutal. Solitary confinement was given to prisoners who broke the rules—locked in a freezing cold dungeon with rations every three days. Eddie was on the receiving end of such punishment on more than one occasion, and it was during one of his stints in solitary that he was abruptly removed and marched into one of the many offices in Fort de Romainville.

Here, Eddie was met by an SS officer, who brutally interrogated him on every aspect of his life prior to his imprisonment. Eddie reeled off a catalogue of his crimes while ensuring that he spent a good amount of time describing his ability with explosives, perhaps out of some sense of pride or a disguised boast of usefulness. After what felt like forever and a day, Eddie was released from the office and taken back to his cell. His time in solitary was over.

Once back in his cell, he spoke with Faramus about the day's events. Faramus was less enthusiastic about their situation than Eddie, as it was clear Eddie may possess a use to the German forces. Faramus, however, realised that they obviously had little use for him; otherwise, he would have also been taken for interrogation. This only became more apparent as more important Nazi party members came to speak with Eddie over time, often on subjects such as his ability to speak German and his motivations to betray his own country.

On one occasion, Eddie enquired as to whether they could use Faramus in addition to himself. With little regard, Eddie was informed that his friend would be remaining in Fort de Romainville as insurance to ensure that Eddie returned from his mission. After four interrogations and several photographs, Eddie was taken from his cell in April 1942. He said goodbye to Anthony Faramus, trying his best to feign enthusiasm. Faramus tried to return the favour, but his despair was obvious.

He was taken to an office, and all his possessions were returned to him, what little that there were. Eddie was allowed to dress himself and was told that from now on he couldn't speak English anymore, only German. He was driven to a villa in Nantes, the location where Eddie Chapman's career as a spy would begin.

The villa Eddie was staying in was unlike anything he had seen before. In the past, he had stayed in some of the nicest hotels money could buy, but the villa in Nantes had something that money couldn't buy: class, and natural beauty. In every direction, stunning landscapes boasting woodlands and rivers overwhelmed him. When he went to sleep that night, it was as though he had never experienced a proper bed before. He may as well not have—he had been in prison for three years and hadn't slept in a proper bed since he broke out two years previous. He had spent his most recent prison time in a concentration camp consisting of conditions beyond human comprehension. He woke up the next morning with a feeling of elation, but despite the somewhat luxurious conditions, he was still focused on escaping back to England.

Eddie may have had moments of doubt, unsure of who was actually on the right side, but in his heart of hearts he knew that when the opportunity arose he was going to do what he believed was the right thing. However, he knew better than to take advantage of the hospitality that the Germans were offering him. Firstly, it would look suspicious if he didn't indulge during his new lifestyle, and secondly, it had been so long since he had been regularly and properly fed that he didn't think he could refuse anything if he wanted to.

It was on the first morning that Eddie spent at the villa that he was informed of the real reason he had been summoned there. He was there to be trained. The first techniques on his assigned curriculum were wireless operation, parachuting, and sabotage. He was fairly confident that he would have no trouble with the sabotage portion of the training in particular—after all, he had made his name as part of the Jelly Gang blowing up safes with gelignite. The other techniques, however, might prove a little challenging.

Eddie was told that he would be tested in all these areas following completion of his training, and if successful, he would be sent on a mission to Britain. He knew there was a financial reward at the end of the missions, but he also detected an implied threat if he didn't manage to pass the tests. Above all of this, even above his desire to get back home, was the knowledge that Anthony Faramus was left behind in the horrors of the concentration camp. It was clear that Anthony's life depended on Eddie's success. This ensured that Eddie was wholly dedicated to soaking up every piece of information from his trainers—every little trick, every minor piece of knowledge. Eddie was given three months to reach the standard they required.

Whilst in jail, Eddie had managed to teach himself to speak French. Such an ambitious task wasn't easy, but Eddie's dedication ensured he achieved what he aimed for. Knowing that such passion and drive existed somewhere inside him, he was sure that he could carry out what was asked of him by the German forces. What Eddie didn't know, however, was that his recruitment was part of a much bigger plan than collecting information to help with the German war effort. Germany had been searching for a British spy for a long time, as they needed as much intel as possible prior to their intended invasion of British shores. The villa in Naples served as their elite training centre, where they intended to turn Eddie Chapman into the kind of spy that Ian Fleming would have been proud of.

Eddie was told that he could explore the surrounding area as long as he had a minder with him. If he came across a local resident, he was instructed to speak only German. His cover story was that he was born in Germany but raised in America by his German mother. He began to explore the local area with the enthusiasm of a small child, as it was a kind of freedom he hadn't felt in many years.

The crash course in espionage took hold quickly. Every day Eddie would engage in bomb-making practices, sending Morse code messages, and jumping out of trees. The physical aspect of the training was difficult to Eddie; he had spent the previous three years hardly being fed, with the concentration camp time being especially hard on him. He was malnourished and out of shape, so he embarked on an exercise regime that slowly-but-surely led him back down the path of physical fitness.

Each day brought a lot of information. His trainers were some of the best spies and saboteurs that the German army had to offer. Unlike other branches of the German secret service, those training him were not amateurs, and it didn't take long for Eddie to learn their ways. He had a natural ability to soak up information quickly, and this shone through in his work. He especially excelled in explosives, which was unsurprising considering his career before he was jailed.

Over time, Eddie developed a solid rapport with his trainers. Although there was considerable joviality on show, Eddie was under no illusions about his situation. He knew that any attempt at escape and he wouldn't be offered a second chance. It was plainly obvious that he was a prisoner, albeit a prisoner with an enjoyable and privileged existence. Eddie didn't intend to make the same mistakes he had in prison before; therefore, there would be no escape attempt until he was on British soil.

By the summer of 1942, the training was going so well that an ex-Gestapo officer attempted to take Chapman away for a month to do some field work, but his handler steadfastly refused. He had no intention of losing his prize asset, especially as he was the first British spy they had managed to attain. By July, Eddie was ready to attempt parachuting properly. Up to now, he had only attempted jumping from trees. His first jump was to be from 900 feet in the air, not a huge distance in terms of parachute jumps, but still significantly higher than Eddie had ever attempted. The 30-foot-high trees he was accustomed to jumping from were a far sight lower.

They chose a clear evening and, after a grandiose dinner at a local restaurant, they drove to an airfield to carry out the jump. Unsurprisingly, the 900-foot jump was a complete success. Not only did it go perfectly, but Eddie felt an incredible exhilaration during the experience. The plane landed, ready for another attempt, this time from 1500 feet. Eddie prepared himself, and when he was given the signal, he jumped without hesitation.

However, as he fell through the air, something didn't go as planned. The parachute hadn't opened properly, and his falling speed was significantly higher than the first attempt. A ferocious blast of icy wind hit the parachute while he was less than 100 feet from the ground. It threw Eddie completely off balance, and he landed face first onto the runway, instantly rendering him unconscious and forcefully removing several of his teeth in the process. The sparkling smile that Eddie often used as an ice breaker when charming young ladies was gone forever.

When he woke up, he was checked out by a doctor and given the all clear. He had been fortunate that, despite essentially falling from an airplane, the parachute had deployed enough to take a lot of the speed out of his fall. He had hit the ground hard, but the damage was superficial. His face would heal, and the work of a good dentist could replace his teeth.

Eddie continued his training once he had fully recovered, focusing heavily on his wireless communication skills. He became proficient in Morse code to the point that he would attempt humour with the operators on the receiving end, although his British sense of humour was wasted on his German counterparts. Perhaps one of the strangest messages ever sent during wartime, Eddie boasted to his German colleagues of his adopted pig.

Unknown to the Germans, their codes that they used to encrypt their messages had been cracked by the cipher experts at Bletchley Park. A little-known fact is that most of the codebreakers at Bletchley Park were female, making up almost three-quarters of the various mathematics, engineering, science, and language experts at the ten-thousand strong workforce. It was these women who intercepted, decoded, and translated the following vital message from a German operator to Eddie Chapman:

'Dear France. Your friend Bobby the Pig grows fatter every day. He is gorging now like a king, roars like a lion, and shits like an elephant. Fritz.'

While Fritz was only the codename that had been assigned to Eddie, the British intelligence were aware that the Germans had a new spy and had been intercepting messages from Nantes for a significant amount of time. There was a distinct worry that he was an Englishman, but they didn't know for sure. It was never suggested that it could be Eddie Chapman. Despite Eddie's infamy before the war, he had become a forgotten figure in the wake of new enemies.

The British army had more important things to worry about, or at least they thought. In terms of breaking the enigma code and cracking the messages that the Germans sent, the British army had the upper hand. Germany, under the impression that their code was unbreakable, were totally unaware that their messages had been intercepted and cracked.

Eddie was the jewel in the crown of German intelligence, but the British intelligence knew all about him, and they intended to steal him. The suspicion that 'Fritz' was English was enough for MI5 to begin plans to utilise him as a double agent when he landed in England. All they needed to do now was wait for the information to be passed on, and they would be ready to strike.

Eddie wasn't ready yet, though. He had excelled with his training so far and had managed to become as proficient as the men teaching him. During the summer months of 1942, he was transferred from Nantes to Berlin, the heart of the German operation. Eddie's handlers were nervous about the movement, as they knew that if anyone found out Eddie was English there was a good chance they would be shot before they had a chance to offer an explanation. Despite their lofty position within the German intelligence agency, there was still a degree of distrust amongst the German army.

Eddie was being transferred to train under Dr Akkerman, an explosives expert. If training in Nantes was high school, then this was a jump equivalent to a master's degree. Eddie was taught an incredible number of techniques, not just in creating explosive devices, but in hiding them from view as well. He spent five days under the tutelage of Dr Akkerman, wherein he learned more than he had in the entire three months at Nantes. When the doctor was happy with Eddie's progress, he was transferred back to Nantes to meet up once again with his chief handler.

It was at this point that Eddie began to feel less than satisfied with his life as a trainee spy. He was beginning to feel guilty about leaving Anthony Faramus, so he asked if he could write to him. However, he was refused. Eddie was told that Faramus would be sent a food parcel at his request, but Eddie said that he wanted to return to Fort de Romainville so he could see his friend in person. His German handlers knew that time was running out; they had to get him to carry out a mission or risk losing him. The wheels were set in motion for Eddie to become the first English spy that the German army had ever created.

In August 1942, Eddie was summoned to the office of his handler. Here, he was handed a contract to sign. He was slightly perplexed by this, as signing a contract to be a spy seemed odd to him. He didn't see how a contract had any more hold over him than the implied threat to Faramus' life. However, Eddie signed the contract without sharing these thoughts with his German handlers. The contract included the amount of money Eddie would receive while he was carrying out his tasks. Once he had signed the contract, the plan was relayed to him: he would parachute into England, gather as large an amount of explosives as he possibly could, and blow up the factory that made the aircraft known as the Mosquito.

The Mosquito was possibly the most versatile aircraft that the British forces owned. It was light, fast, and easy to manufacture, and it could carry out a number of different tasks. Eddie's taking out the De Havilland factory where it was created would gain the German army a slight upper hand in the war. There was also the fact that Eddie's handlers were desperate to show that their training school was worth persisting with. If Eddie could carry out this job, then he would be proving his worth and by extension that of the continued funding of the villa in Nantes.

Eddie had to make one trip back to Dr Akkerman before he was ready to make his flight. Dr Akkerman went through a thorough recap of all the skills that he had taught to Eddie, then went over the correct way to blow up the De Havilland factory. Once the doctor was satisfied with Eddie's explosive prowess, he was sent back to Nantes.

As soon as the date was set, Eddie was given enough money to survive and carry out his task, in addition to a variety of tricks and tools to both help him complete his mission and return word to Germany regarding the status. Mundford in Norfolk was chosen as his landing spot for its small rural population, and he was ready to fly. Things changed in November, much to Eddie's dismay. Hitler had changed his war plans and decided that taking over the whole of France was the best plan of action. This meant that Eddie and the rest of the people deployed at the Nantes villa were all drafted into the German army to help with the occupation.

Eddie was taken on a raid to flush out possible French resistance members, but all he ended up doing was breaking down some doors and getting drunk. Eddie was in a state of flux; he had enjoyed the whole episode. He felt slightly guilty about this but didn't let it get to him. He knew that once he was back in Nantes, the plans would be rearranged, and he would be back in England. Then, he could go about finding a way to escape the clutches of the Germans. It came faster than he expected—the drop was planned for the 16th of December 1942. Eddie was to be back home for Christmas. At first, all he could think about was seeing his daughter and making contact with the various women from his life. Then, the gravity of the situation dawned on him. In fact, he had no idea what he was going to do when he got to England.

His mission was still to sabotage the De Havilland factory, but Eddie also had to ensure that he made contact with the Germans each day. Failure to do so would lead to them assuming he had been captured or defected back to the British side. Eddie was informed that if the De Havilland job was too difficult, then he should attempt to sabotage a number of factories in the area that made parts for the British fighter planes. While the De Havilland factory was his primary target, Eddie was told that he should just generally cause as much trouble as he could without getting caught. He was also there to complete an intelligence mission by gathering as much information he could about the movement of US troops. The Americans had been barely part of the war when Eddie was recruited by the Germans, but they were starting to have more of an impact. A lot of their soldiers were deployed to England to help fight off any potential invasion, as most English soldiers were spread out around the world fighting on different fronts. Eddie had a wide range of responsibilities to carry out, but none of them worried him. His only aim when he landed was to find a way to make himself known to the

British secret service without tipping off the Germans. Eddie was told he had three months to carry out his mission, and then he should return through Portugal, which at the time was a neutral zone.

Before Eddie flew out, he was searched to ensure that there was nothing on his person that could identify him as a German spy, then he was packed off with his medley of tools and money to board the plane that would fly him over Mundford.

By late 1942, Eddie Chapman was officially a spy and on his way to his first mission.

Chapter 4: Double Agent

Eddie Chapman stepped onto the Focke-Wulf that was going to take him back home with a sense of trepidation. Although this was the moment he had been looking forward to for months, the nerves of it all had been taking over. As the plane took off towards England, though, his nerves subsided somewhat. He found it strange that other occupants of the plane were so jovial. The British Isles were known to shine spotlights searching for German aircraft during the night. This might not be a bombing raid, but the British military wouldn't know that. There was nothing to stop them from being shot down if their craft was spotted. This naturally concerned Eddie, evidently more than the other passengers on the plane. Perhaps it was because of their experience that they weren't worried, or perhaps it was he who was the one doing the drop, which meant his nerves were jangling more than the others. Whatever the reason, Eddie found it difficult to relax, and his concentration greatly suffered for it.

When it finally came time for him to jump, a slight issue arose. His backpack was overly large due to the amount of supplies and tools he needed for his mission, causing it to get caught on the hatch in the plane. Eddie was lodged in place, panicking as the plane sliced through the air at incredible speeds. A swift boot into his back caused him to become dislodged and, before he could process what happened, Eddie was pirouetting through the sky at an astounding rate. He dropped quickly and landed without incident, but what Eddie didn't know was that he had landed around 20 miles away from his target in Mundford.

Something else he didn't know was that the British intelligence were already perfectly aware of his arrival. They were in a difficult situation when it came to the landing of the German spy. They knew exactly when he would be landing and had a rough idea on where it would be, but their hands were tied regarding capturing him. There was no full computer database digitally linked across the world during this era, meaning that even though they knew what his fake identities were, they had no way of guaranteeing they would be recognised by the right sources. They couldn't put out any kind of bulletin, as this would alert the Germans to their messages not just being intercepted but also deciphered. Any kind of large-scale search operation would have the same effect. They had to rely on blind luck.

Fortunately, none of this really mattered, because Eddie

Chapman intended to take the luck of the situation out of their hands.

Eddie stumbled around the dark countryside for hours. He had lost his map—not that it would have helped him much, as he wasn't where he had expected to land, due to the brief time that he had spent stuck in the hatch of the plane. Finally, after almost four hours, he came across a farm. He was worried at this time that he may have landed in France, such was his disorientation. He ran up to the farmhouse and banged aggressively on the front door. A lady shouted out to him asking who was there, and he concocted a story about being a British airman.

Once inside, he sat down and asked if he could use the farm owner's phone to call the police. The lady's husband phoned them directly for him, and Eddie gave them as much information as he could. Once the police arrived, he surrendered his weapon to them and told them that he needed to see the British Intelligence Service. He was taken back to the police station, where he was searched more thoroughly.

While Eddie kept insisting that he needed to see the intelligence service, the Deputy Chief Constable probed for more information. Eddie never lost his cool and maintained his stance of telling them as little as possible. Some questions he told them were only for the intelligence service to hear, and he actively stopped them from opening his bag containing his wireless radio. Eddie was much less nervous than he had been on the plane. He wondered to himself if it was the parachute jump that had worried him more than the actual espionage.

It didn't take long for the intelligence service to arrive. Two men pulled up in a black car, signed the relevant papers, then took Eddie to London. Here, he was detained and dressed in prison clothes before a doctor came to give him a thorough physical. This wasn't just to ensure that Eddie was in good condition physically—the intelligence service had managed to obtain enough information about Eddie from intercepting German radio talk that they even knew details of his dental records. The physical gave them the opportunity to find out if the man who had turned himself in was the German spy known as Fritz.

Eddie was cleared medically, and then he had his photo taken from several different angles, all while he was unsure what was going to happen to him. No one had informed him of anything up to this point. As far as he knew, he had been captured and was going to be treated as a traitor. However, he still wasn't worried. He had turned himself in and had enough information to barter his way out of trouble. Eddie knew there was no way he would be executed, especially not before they had found out what he knew. He also knew that the potential to find out more information would be hard for the intelligence service to resist.

Eddie was about to find out that he was to be interrogated by the best that the British Intelligence Service had to offer, an officer named Colonel Robin Stephens. He had checked on Eddie briefly when he arrived but had said nothing to the new prisoner. Once Eddie had been thoroughly examined, he intended to extract all the information that he could from him. He was a skilled interrogator and used a technique very similar to the good cop, bad cop routine that is so common in modern police procedural shows. It was apparent as soon as the interrogation began that any such techniques wouldn't be needed. Eddie Chapman was more than happy to give up any and all information that he could recall. He gladly shared everything that he could remember about his time in Nantes as well as his handlers from the villa. Eddie told them everything, from his youth and beginnings as a small-time crook to where he was at that moment. During a break in the interrogation, Colonel Stephens took a phone call from the police officer who had responded first to the call from the farmhouse that Eddie had stumbled upon. He told the colonel that he had served with Eddie in the Coldstream Guards. The information that he relayed about this experience tallied up with everything that Eddie had told them about that period in his life.

Here, Eddie was allowed a break, and he needed it due to physical and mental exhaustion. Once he had eaten and rested up, he was immediately taken back to the interrogation room. It was here that he revealed the codes to crack the German encryptions.

This was incredible information for the British Intelligence Service. It showed them that not only had their efforts to crack the code been completely correct, but the Germans were still unaware that their code had been uncovered. Eddie gave up information from every facet of his life, even revealing his experimentation with homosexuality earlier in his younger years. He gave up all the names of the people whom he had come across during his time training, but it was apparent to the British Intelligence that these were all pseudonyms. They mentioned the real names of his handlers, but this garnered no reaction from Eddie. He didn't know their real names, just the names he had been told. The British Intelligence knew who they were from the descriptions that Eddie had given them. After nearly two days of almost continuous interrogation, Eddie's stress continually intensified. He needed to make contact with his German spymasters or they would begin to suspect that things had gone wrong.

He wrote a letter to Colonel Stephens informing him that while he was more than willing to cooperate as a double agent and had, in fact, come to them with that intention, he found it amusing that the Germans, the enemy, had treated him with warmth and kindness while his own country gave him a prison cell and interrogation. The British intelligence officers were busy debating what to do with Eddie Chapman. He had a long, sordid career as a criminal, but he was seemingly willing to carry out several dangerous tasks for his country. They acknowledged that he had already carried out a risky manoeuvre by turning himself in. Colonel Stephens gave his opinion that Eddie was genuine and wanted to fight for his country, to do the right thing. The other members of the committee agreed. A case officer was sent to give Eddie the once over, and by the evening of the 18th of December, more than two days after Eddie had landed back in Britain, he was given the codename Agent Zigzag.

Chapter 5: Being Agent Zigzag

Eddie was assigned Captain Ronnie Reed as his new handler. The moment the two men were introduced, Ronnie was informed that he had to supervise Eddie in relaying his message to the Germans. It was Ronnie's job to make sure that the message Eddie sent back wasn't giving the Germans any kind of information that could give away what was happening. Once the two men had met and spoke for a while, Ronnie informed Eddie that he would be returning tomorrow to send the message, and he should have a think about what exactly he wanted to say, then they would write out the message together.

The next day, Ronnie and two police officers picked up Eddie to take him to a suitable place to relay his message. He chose an equestrian club with a large flagpole that he thought could be used as an aerial. Once they had everything set up,

Eddie relayed his message:

'FFFFF HAVE ARRIVED. AM WELL WITH FRIENDS. OK. HI HU HA.'

The strange flourish at the end of the message was a little idiosyncrasy that Eddie had developed while learning how to use the wireless equipment. He felt that it encapsulated his personality well as it gave the impression of laughter. It also helped when sending his message as it convinced the Germans on the receiving end that it was indeed him. The five instances of the letter f at the start of his message conveyed to the Germans that everything was okay. If he started his message with five instances of the letter p then that was code to let them know that he was being followed by the police or other security forces. In addition to these two codes, if he started his message without either of them then it was code to let them know that he had been captured and was being forced to send messages by whomever had captured him. The following day, Eddie and Ronnie couldn't establish contact with Paris again. They could only make contact with Nantes, where Eddie had been trained. He informed them that he couldn't get through to Paris and hadn't gotten a reply for over a week.

All the while he was communicating with the Germans, he was still giving British intelligence a steady stream of information. They were shocked at just how much he could remember from what he had seen. It didn't take them long to realise that they had something special on their hands. If they could keep Eddie Chapman happy, then they had a double agent who could provide them with a trove of important information. The first step towards this was to move Eddie out of his prison cell into a more comfortable setting. British intelligence used two of their best officers to act as a chaperone for Eddie while they took him to a safehouse. The intention was to make Eddie feel comfortable and at home, while also keeping him out of the hands of his old criminal friends. They were given money to take him to the pub now and then, and Eddie himself was given cash so he could get his round in.

Although both men were directed to behave as friends to Eddie, they were also given guns and instructed never to leave him alone. If he tried to escape, they were to restrain him. Eddie was no slouch when it came to pugilistic arts, but he had nothing on the two men who had been charged with watching over him. The house that they were to live in was a three-bedroom one. The back bedroom was designated as the radio room; an aerial had been attached to the chimney the day before they arrived. Eddie took the middle room, and the third bedroom was shared by Eddie's two companions. The two officers decided to divide up the task of monitoring what Eddie said and did. The first man, Allan Tooth, kept observations on Eddie's personality, and the second man,

Paul Backwell, made a record of the factual information that Eddie gave them. Eddie didn't know that they were spying on him as well, and it only took a few days before he was completely comfortable with his two companions.

Throughout this time, Eddie was having trouble communicating with the Germans. The radio didn't seem to work as well as it should. It was picking up minor snippets here and there, but it could never seem to get a full-strength signal. Ronnie Reed felt that he was pretty well versed in the usage of wireless radios but could find nothing wrong with it each time he checked it out. It was only when Eddie informed him that he had fixed a loose connection in the back with a hot poker as a soldering iron that he realised what the problem might be. Ronnie took the wireless home with him and fixed it properly, ensuring that everything was mended. He brought it back to Eddie the next morning with the wireless in perfect working order.

Eddie had Ronnie check over his message, and on the 27th of December 1942 he transmitted: *'CALL AT 1000 IF PARIS UNABLE TO RECEIVE ME. OK FRITZ. HU HA HU HO.'* The message went through without a hitch, and Ronnie and Eddie retired to the kitchen for a cup of tea. It was here that the realisation of what he had done dawned on him. Eddie turned to Ronnie and said: *'My God, I believe I forgot the Fs.'*

The uproar within the British Intelligence Service was a

marvel to behold. Ronnie Reed was admonished in a manner that he had never experienced before. He stammered out his excuses, but none of them really made any headway with his superiors. It was mainly because he didn't believe them himself—he knew that he had made a terrible mistake. By missing the Fs off the start of the message it sent the signal to the Germans that Eddie had been compromised by the British Intelligence Service. They had gone from having the most promising double agent they had ever come across to potentially having nothing in a matter of moments. After the mistake had been realised they had sent another message later in the evening saying: *'FFFFF SORRY DRUNK OVER XMAS FORGOT FFFFF. HAPPY XMAS. F.'* Ronnie explained to his superior that he was hopeful that they would believe the second message, and everything would be okay. He reminded them that it was perfectly possible that Eddie would have forgotten to put the five Fs at the start even if he hadn't defected to their side. It still did nothing to placate his superiors, and it didn't ease his conscience either. Ronnie was an experienced wireless operator. Some would even describe him as an expert. He shouldn't be making elementary mistakes like this.

It wasn't just the fear of losing Eddie that was upsetting the British intelligence. This mistake could tip off the Germans to other double agents that they had working for them. The radio traffic operators finally managed to intercept a message conveying that the Germans had believed Eddie's second message. Once this news was broke, the collective sigh of relief was a big one. Despite this lucky break, Eddie was starting to show signs of ill temper and even depression. The root of his upset was his daughter. She was three years old by this point, and Eddie had never even met her, let alone held her in his arms. He was feeling more and more upset about the situation with each passing day. This wasn't helped by the Germans, who were starting to press Eddie for more information. Not only had he agreed to sabotage the De Havilland aircraft factory, but he had also said he would gather information about government buildings and American troop movements. That he hadn't managed to carry out the sabotage yet wasn't a big deal to the Germans—they understood that it wasn't an easy job and would take time— but the troop movements and other information should have been easy work for him. He informed Ronnie of this, and they set about making a plan to give as much information as possible without giving away anything too crucial.

Eddie and his two handlers were to go shopping in the West End of London. During this trip, Eddie was to try and spot anything that he could possibly use as information to pass to the Germans. This way he would be giving them legitimate information but without leaking anything too important to the war effort. Everyone was on board with the plan, and during his trips out, Eddie was back to his old self. Happy and jovial. However, the darkness descended on him once more when he got back to the safe house. His mind drifted back to Freda and his daughter. He desperately wanted to see them, and he started asking Ronnie at regular intervals to try and facilitate a meeting for him. It was in between these regular requests that Eddie outlined his plan to assassinate Hitler. While Ronnie thought it was absurd, Eddie had the utmost confidence in his own ability to get the job done. Eddie told Ronnie that his German handlers would be able to get him a front row seat at one of Hitler's rallies, and then from there it would just be a case of using his skill with explosives to take out Hitler as well as a large number of prominent members of the Nazi party. Eddie said that he knew he would never be able to adjust to a life without crime—at least this way he could give his life some meaning.

Ronnie secretly admired Eddie's dedication to going out big, but they never discussed the plan again. Eddie never brought it up again because his energy was solely devoted to his wish to see Freda and his daughter. He devoted his time to asking his two companions and Ronnie if they would organise a meeting for him. Eddie thought that it would solve all the issues in his head; Ronnie wasn't so sure. He didn't know if Freda would react positively to seeing Eddie, and he didn't want to plunge him even deeper into a pit of despair.

During his time at Nantes, Eddie had been blown away by

the level of efficiency that the Germans had shown. Everything was timed to perfection and planned out down to the last detail. It felt that things had fallen apart since he left them. On the 14th of January 1943, Eddie received a message that he should send his messages blind and into the ether due to the technical difficulties that they were facing at their end. Eddie found this incredibly annoying. Perhaps it was his way of unleashing the frustration he was feeling about Freda and his daughter, but the message that he sent back was not a pleasant one. He let them have it with a barrage of fury:

'FFFFF DISGUSTED AND WORRIED BY LACK OF RECEPTION. THIS IS A HOPELESS BUNGLE. HAVE BEEN PROMISED FULL SUPPORT AND MUST HAVE IT. WORK GOING SPLENDIDLY. HAVE FULL LIST OF ALL YOU WANT. YOU MUST DO SOMETHING TO CLEAR UP THE TROUBLE. F.'

Once Eddie had sent his borderline-abusive message to the Germans, the British Intelligence Service monitored the radio waves for the fallout. There was nothing. It soon became apparent that the underlings had suppressed the message to spare themselves the wrath of their superiors. Ronnie Reed began to wonder if he should have done the same himself when Eddie had forgotten his call sign but thought better of mentioning it. It didn't take the Germans long to fix their transmission errors, and from then on, Eddie was always able to get in touch easily each time.

As soon as the wireless transmission was fixed, the next step of the double agent plan was put into action. Eddie was taken into London to purchase the materials he needed to make a bomb—the bomb that would have been used to sabotage the De Havilland aircraft factory. While the Intelligence Service had no intention of allowing Eddie to actually blow it up, they needed to make sure that the materials were available in London; otherwise, the Germans could have found out that Eddie was lying about making the bomb. Eddie practiced making a bomb on a small scale but didn't test it out. His handlers felt that wartime Britain was definitely not the place to be testing out a homemade bomb in a rear garden. Now they had managed to make sure that the materials could be sourced, they had to think of a way to make it look like the aircraft factory had been bombed and to get the news out there so that the Germans would find out independently of Eddie. There was just two things standing in their way of having Eddie completely on board.

Freda, and Freda and Eddie's daughter.

It was all that Eddie spoke about. All he wanted was to look after his child and, to a lesser extent, reconnect with Freda. He had enquired about Betty Farmer at one point, but she had managed to go completely off the grid, a trick made far easier by the outbreak of war and the lack of computerised databases. Ronnie and his superiors began to discuss trying to bring Freda and the child to Eddie. They knew that Eddie was vitally important to the war effort, and if they didn't have him at his best, it could seriously impede his performance. The decision was made to get in touch with her and sound out the possibility of her coming to stay with Eddie at the safe house. She was told that he had been freed from the Jersey prison on the condition that he would join the army and be posted overseas. She believed the story, or at least pretended to, without any questions. She wanted to see Eddie almost as much as he wanted to see her. They all met at a hotel just outside London on the 26th of January, where Eddie related to her the same story. The next day, Freda and their daughter, Diane, moved into the safe house with Eddie.

The effect on Eddie was instant. He was immediately more dedicated to his task. There were obstacles that had to be avoided, such as the daily messages that Eddie had to send to the Germans. They had to be sent at 9:45 a.m. each day. This meant that Freda had to be kept away from Eddie at this time so that he could send the message. It required a slight negotiation on the part of Eddie and his handlers, but fortunately for them, Freda was an accommodating person and always left Eddie to his tasks without complaint or question.

Eddie had a reason to live again. He no longer desired to spend time in the company of prostitutes; when he wasn't working, he just wanted to be with Freda and Diane. He told Ronnie that he wanted to complete the De Havilland fake sabotage as soon as possible. His enthusiasm for his work was only matched by his joy at having his family in his life.

The British Intelligence Service hadn't just brought Freda and Diane into Eddie's life out of the kindness of their hearts. There were methodical reasons behind it. They knew that Eddie was much less likely to defect to the Germans if he had his family waiting for him back home. It may have been seen as a risk to bring Freda back into Eddie's life, but from their point of view, it was a calculated one. Eddie never realised the reasoning behind their change of heart, but it was a similar emotional tool to the one the Germans had used with Anthony Faramus—although significantly less sinister and deceitful.

What Eddie didn't know was that during his time in Nantes and England, Anthony Faramus had been transferred to a death camp. The Germans had forgotten about him, and he had fallen through the cracks.

The fake destruction of the De Havilland factory was causing the British Intelligence Service a great deal of trouble. They didn't want to actually destroy the factory, for obvious reasons, but at the same time, they knew that if it didn't look genuine then the Germans would be onto Eddie in an instant. As well as being on to Eddie, they knew that it would tip them off about the goings on at Bletchley Park too. This had to be done right, for both Eddie's and the British war effort's sake.

To make sure that they created a believable illusion, they took the surprising step of bringing in an actual illusionist. He wasn't just any run-of-the-mill illusionist, either. He was a semi-famous magician named Jasper Maskelyne. Jasper had been part of the war effort from the start, initially just used to entertain the troops. It wasn't until a forward-thinking general thought that his skills could be used for deception that he was brought into actual conflict.

Sent to North Africa, he spearheaded an ingenious scheme that saw the Germans ignoring the British Army and succumbing to a surprise attack, all because Jasper and his crew had built a fake water pipeline and two thousand fake tanks. They used this to make the Germans think that an attack couldn't possibly be launched before November due to the half-finished state of the water pipeline. Once the high-ranking German officials took leave, the British attacked near the end of October. As an expert in such deceptions, Jasper was the perfect person to call for this job.

Jasper got right to work formulating a plan. His first idea, however, was quickly vetoed by the British Intelligence Service. He wanted to set fire to asbestos boards laid on the roof of the building, but the British felt that this would provide a target for any potential bombings, so the idea was scrapped. His second plan was to cover various elements of the factory with painted tarpaulin. The tarpaulin was to be painted to look as though it was either holes in the ground or broken walls.

From up close it may not fool anyone, but from any kind of distance it would look utterly convincing, at least for both airborne surveillance and any double agents in the area who passed by to check. Jasper decided to supplement this with models of the sub-transformers inside the factory. By rolling them onto their side around the site and hiding the real ones with a painted tarpaulin, it would look as though they had been blown up. The gates were replaced with twisted versions and black soot was spread around the whole site. Jasper had made De Havilland look as though a bomb had hit it. It was perfect. All the scheme needed now was Eddie to do his side of things.

Eddie sent a message to the Germans informing them of his intention to carry out the sabotage. The camouflaging of the factory was to take place on the night of the 29th of January, as this provided the darkest night for the illusionists to work without being spotted. Eddie fired up his wireless and tapped out his message: *'FFFFF WALTER READY TO GO. BEGIN PREPARATIONS FOR MY RETURN. F.'* Then, the British had to find a way to get the information into newspapers. After they were rebuffed by the *Times*, it was finally the *Express* that agreed to publish a small paragraph about the factory attack. Worried about what the wartime censors would say about a story that could encourage the enemy, it was agreed that it would only go out in the first edition. The plans were laid and set. All that was needed now was for Eddie to confirm the date of the attack to his German handlers, and everything would be good to go. He set up his wireless again to send one more message before the task was undertaken: *'FFFFF ARRANGEMENTS FOR WALTER ARE NOW COMPLETE. OBJECTIVES ARE SUBSTATIONS.'* With that final message, everything was in place.

Once all of the preparations had been made, it was time for Eddie to inform the Germans that he had carried out the task. He fired up his wireless and sent the message: *'FFFFF WALTER BLOWN IN TWO PLACES.'* This got a jubilant reply from the German side *'CONGRATULATIONS ON GOO RESULT OF WALTER. PLEASE SEND INFO ON NEWSPAPER REPORTS. WILL DO ALL WE CAN ARRANGE YOUR RETURN. STATE PROPOSITIONS.'* The newspaper report took up a meagre three lines and was printed in the first edition at 5:00 a.m.

The news of the bombing was greeted with even more cheer by the Germans after Berlin was hit by a bombing raid by a squadron of Mosquitos. Eddie had proven himself to be a reliable and useful asset to the Germans, which made him even more useful to the British. The British were intent on sending him back to France as soon as possible. They knew that the longer he was in England, the more likely it was that the police would catch on to him being there. If it got out that a known criminal was being harboured, it wouldn't take long for the Germans to find out that Eddie had been turned.

After a brief sojourn to meet with the head of MI5's explosives division, Eddie was back at the safe house waiting for his next orders. Freda took Diane for a walk while Tar Robinson, the head of the double agent program, outlined what he required next from Eddie. Robinson informed Eddie that he would be returning to France to work as a long-term double agent. His job would be to gather information on the Germans' own espionage program to aid the weeding out and subsequent turning of German spies. Eddie was told to discover information without trying too hard to find it. The British Intelligence Service didn't want Eddie to do anything that would give him away to the Germans; they just wanted him to take things easy and pass on any information that he found out naturally. As well as this, he wasn't to use a wireless to send messages back. They knew that it would be too easy to intercept these messages and totally blow his cover. Despite their trust that Eddie wouldn't purposely betray them, they knew that if the Germans found out that he was acting as a double agent then there was no way that Eddie could withstand their interrogation methods.

Eddie was told that there was a cover story being prepared for him that was as close to the truth as possible. This was to ensure that he didn't get caught up in his own lies and could tell the truth where possible. The problem that was facing Eddie and his handlers was that the Germans were in no great rush to get him back to France.

After the last message that Eddie had received, which asked him to state propositions, he decided to send them a message with some suggestions on how he could get back: *'FFFFF PICK UP BY SUBMARINE OR SPEEDBOAT. WILL FIND SUITABLE POINT ON COAST. TRYING TO GET SHIPS PAPERS. SEE BACK PAGE EXPRESS FEB 1.'* With this message, Eddie both conveyed his desire to be picked up by the Germans, rather than taking a more hazardous journey through Portugal, as well as where they could find the information about the bombings in the newspapers. Eddie was dismayed at the reply he received *'IMPOSSIBLE PICK YOU UP BY SUBMARINE. RETURN NORMAL WAY.'* It was evident that the Germans had no intention of picking up Eddie. If he was to get back to France, he would have to make his own way via Lisbon. This was something that both Eddie and the British intended to avoid if possible. If Eddie was to make his own way back to France, he would have no protection as he did so. It was a big risk, but it was also a risk for him to remain in Britain. The British Intelligence assumed that was because the Germans had no intention of paying him the £15,000 that they had promised him. Eddie had no such thoughts, though. He even made out a will in which he stipulated that the £15,000 be split up between Freda and Diane. Despite his own double dealings, he felt supremely confident that the Germans wouldn't attempt to double cross him.

What Eddie hadn't considered was that British intelligence intended to pay him as well. They knew that it was unfair for them to ask him to risk his life for them without some form of reward, even though he was a wanted criminal. They didn't tell him about this and invested the money they paid him into a three per cent war loan held in a savings account at the local co-op. The irony of holding money for Eddie Chapman in a co-op didn't escape anyone, but this time he was legally making money through them. The money was to be paid to Eddie upon his final return at the end of the war, and in the case of his untimely demise, it was to be given to Freda and Diane to help them to survive without Eddie to provide for them.

There was still no word back from the Germans, and Eddie and Ronnie were starting to become worried. Their apathy to his situation was a warning sign that they intended to try and keep Eddie there for as long as possible. They decided to try a ruse to force their hand. Eddie had already informed the Germans that he had used his old Jelly Gang colleague Jimmy Hunt in the sabotage of the De Havilland factory. He had also tried to swindle an extra £15,000 out of them as 'payment' for Jimmy's help. Eddie knew that he had to forgo that money and use the fictional Jimmy as his fall guy to get them to spring into action. On the 9th of February, Eddie broke off a transmission to the Germans using his danger signal 'PPPPP'. Despite this, there was no change in the demeanour of the Germans. In fact, they seemed utterly unfazed by it all. Eddie and Ronnie were furious and sent another message attempting to cajole the Germans: '*FFFFF DANGEROUS TO CONTINUE TRANSMITTING. THINGS GETTING AWKWARD. ESSENTIAL COME BACK WITH JIMMY. HAVE IMPORTANT DOCUMENTS. SHIPS PAPERS HARD TO OBTAIN.*' Eddie hoped that this would have the desired effect, but once again the pleas for help were ignored. In fact, the Germans just asked for more information about the bombing of the De Havilland factory. Eddie sent them information about the fake bombing and then followed up by asking if they were ready to facilitate his arrival through Portugal. Eddie received no answer to this. Ronnie decided that they would need to employ more devious tactics. On the 12th of February, two separate newspapers had stories planted about gelignite-based arrests being made. While both stories were fake, they still piqued the interest of German intelligence. This was supplemented by Eddie's next message: 'FFFFF JIMMY ARRESTED. SEE EVENING STANDARD FEBRUARY 12TH FRONT PAGE. CLOSING TRANSMITTER AT ONCE. WILL TRY TO GET TO LISBON. FRITZ.' This made the Germans sit up and take notice.

The Germans began frantically searching the airwaves for any trace of their man. That Eddie was now in serious danger, or so they thought, had made them spring into action, even though his repeated warnings hadn't had the desired effect.

This allowed Eddie the clarity of mind to realise that he had hitched his wagon to the right team when he decided to switch sides. The Germans saw him as an asset, and they were only interested now because his being captured would be of grave consequence to them. Freda and Diane were to spend one more night with Eddie before they had to leave. This moment had been expected, as from the start Freda had been told that Eddie would be joining up to fight in the future. They spent their last night together, and Eddie and Ronnie had to get to work. Eddie's story needed to be engraved into his mind.

A full week was spent on drilling the cover story into Eddie's head. Everything from the moment his parachute was deployed up until the moment that Jimmy Hunt was incarcerated was gone over countless times. Eddie was fatigued by it, but he knew that it was a matter of life and death. After a week of study, someone was brought in to interrogate Eddie. He was mentally attacked from the first moment. Questions that Eddie hadn't been prepared for were thrown at him, but Eddie dealt with them both convincingly and accurately. The British secret services were surprised and impressed with Eddie's ability to lie convincingly. If they hadn't known the truth themselves, they would have believed the stories that he was weaving.

After the intelligence service were satisfied that Eddie was in no danger if interrogated, they got down to the task of sorting out the information that was safe to hand over to the

Germans. Eddie reeled off all the information that he had collected that might be of interest to the Germans, and Ronnie and his team cut anything that might be of actual use to them as well as adding false information for the sake of extra deception. The report was infused with disinformation that all had a hint of truth to it. Once the report was complete, Eddie wrote it out onto 14 sheets of paper using the special invisible ink that the Germans had given to him.

Ronnie Reed and MI5 did undertake one deception of their own with Eddie. Before he left, Eddie was informed that they still couldn't crack the German transmissions that they intercepted. Even with the codes that Eddie had provided, they told him, it was still almost impossible to do. This was patently untrue, as Bletchley Park had cracked the German codes a long time ago, but Ronnie wanted to ensure that if Eddie was rumbled as a double agent, then he at least couldn't give away this secret. Eddie believed Ronnie completely, as matched what he had been told by the Germans—that their codes were impenetrable.

Eddie was asked to complete a questionnaire about information he might gather when he was back in France. It covered almost everything that could possibly be thought of, and Eddie was in a confident mood. He filled in the questionnaire like a child choosing sweets in a sweet shop. Eddie believed he could find out anything and everything. In closing, Eddie was told to take up any opportunity given to him. Anything from bringing over a team of saboteurs to training potential new spies could be of value to the British. They knew that with Eddie's skills, anything was possible.

Chapter 6: Returning To The Enemy

The ship that was chosen for Eddie's voyage was the *City of Lancaster*. It was a three-thousand-ton merchant ship that carried a wide variety of cargo, all of it designed to help the Allied war effort. The captain of the ship was met by Ronnie Reed before it set sail. Ronnie briefed the captain that Eddie would be coming aboard as an assistant steward. He wasn't introduced to the captain as Eddie Chapman, though. Eddie had taken on the name and papers of his old Jelly Gang member, Hugh Anson. The captain was informed that Eddie would be travelling as far as Lisbon with them. He understood that this would leave the ship a man down regarding crew, but it really was vital to the war effort that this man was kept safe. Far from being put out that an inexperienced seaman was taking up an important space on his crew, the captain was delighted to be undertaking such an important task.

The cover story for Hugh Anson was that he had been released from prison early on the proviso that he was willing to join the merchant navy. He was introduced to the rest of the crew as a bad egg who intended to make a fresh start. Of course, when he absconded at Lisbon, it could easily be explained away as his still being the same old bad egg he'd always been.

Eddie was to tell the Germans that he had paid the real Hugh Anson £100 for his documents and then replaced the pictures with his own. He was also to tell them that the real Anson had agreed to keep a low profile for a few months before reporting his papers as missing. Eddie and Ronnie also concocted a way for Eddie to communicate with the British without raising the suspicions of his German comrades. As he usually put a laughing flourish at the end of his messages, they devised a way of using them to give information.

Eddie was fully prepared to do his duty while out in France. As Eddie had full access to the *Times* while he was with the Germans, it was agreed that after he had sent a message then a message would be posted in the personals saying, 'Mrs West thanks the anonymous donor for the gift of £38.' The value of the money could vary depending on how many messages were sent, with the second digit of the money letting Eddie know how many messages had been received.

There was also a trap laid out where Eddie would inform the Germans that if any of their spies were in any kind of trouble, they could call Gerrard 4850 and say. 'It's Lew Leibich speaking, and I would like to speak to Jimmy.' Of course, this number wouldn't put them through to any Jimmy—it would go straight to Ronnie Reed, who would then set up a sting operation.

The ship set sail on the 15th of March 1943. In the ship's safe was a package containing Eddie's revolver that the Germans had given him, fully loaded, and £50 in £1 notes. He set about his mission on the boat by complaining loudly about every task that he was given. While he was genuinely annoyed at having to do so much menial work, it was also part of his act as a bad egg. He had managed to convince the captain to keep his papers that contained the invisible ink information in the ship's safe, as well. The captain was more than happy to help but was also bemused by the request.

Eddie did the bare minimum regarding work, so much so that his crew mates were annoyed by him. He did, however, manage to endear himself to them in other ways. Eddie had a natural charisma and charm that instantly made people like him. It was part of the reason why he was such a good spy.

It wasn't his crew mates that were the greatest worry to Eddie. German reconnaissance planes had cottoned on to their path. If they managed to relay the information to the German navy, there was a good chance that there could be attacks on the ships. It didn't matter to them that Eddie was on board, partly because they didn't know he was on board, but also because it was important to stop the flow of supplies for the Allies. Eddie's worst fears were proven right when a group of U-boats attacked the convoy of ships. Luck was shining down on Eddie this day, though. Two merchant ships and a tanker were sunk by the U-boats, but the *City of Lancaster* managed to escape harm. Eddie approached the captain and asked if he could report the position and route that the ships were taking in his notes. He said as the Germans already knew where they were, as shown by the attack, it wouldn't actually give them any new information, but it would be useful for him to show that he was a willing agent. The captain agreed with Eddie's logic, and Eddie set to work writing down his information with his invisible ink.

Other than the attack by the U-boats, Eddie's journey was relatively uneventful. He entertained his crew mates with poems and stories of his misspent youth, all designed to both trigger rumours about him and lend him an air of mystery. Eddie was a complete enigma to the crew, which was just how he liked it. The ship docked in Lisbon on the 18th of March. Eddie had spent three days doing menial work, and he didn't intend to do it again. He spent an evening drinking in a bar before abruptly leaving, telling his friends that he had to meet up with a friend. What they didn't know was that Eddie was on his way to meet with his contact with the Germans.

Eddie was about to encounter some more bad luck, though. The safe house that he was supposed to go to had been burned. It was no longer in use, and it wasn't safe for Eddie to go there. Oblivious to the danger, Eddie made his way there and was greeted with confusion and incredulence. After finally managing to get some form of information from the inhabitants of the house, he was taken to a cafe where a young girl phoned a number for him. Eddie spoke his password down the phone, but it had no effect. The man spoke some French, however, and Eddie managed to organise a meeting with him. The man arrived with another older man in tow. Eddie gave his password again and said that he needed to speak to a senior German officer. He got nothing back but a scared look. Eddie realised that he wasn't helping matters and could, in fact, be putting himself in danger. He told the two men to forget about their meeting and ran away.

Eddie absconded to the arms of a local prostitute for the evening, already forgetting about Freda, and early the next morning he made his way to the German Legation. When he informed the man at the front desk who he was and that he wanted to see senior officials associated with the German espionage program, he was told to come back in two hours. When Eddie returned, an official gave him an address that he would need to visit. Once Eddie got there, he was intercepted by two men in a car and driven to another address. Here, he was asked what his business was and told to identify himself. He gave the story that he had learned by rote before he set sail, and the two men seemed satisfied. They informed him that he was to return to the *City of Lancaster* and then return to the house they were in the next day. Eddie did as he was told and returned to the ship.

Once there, Eddie received the roasting of a lifetime from the captain on the ship. Although it was all an act, the other members of the crew were taken aback by it. They were even more shocked when Eddie talked back to the captain. Eddie Chapman, or Hugh Anson as he was known, was really living up to his reputation as a rebel. Once the men were all out of the way and Eddie and the captain were alone, they spoke about what had happened and began to prepare for Eddie's leaving of the ship. The captain suggested that it would make sense for Eddie to start a fight with another crew member—this way it gave him even more of a reason to abruptly leave the ship, as his cover story dictated that he would be facing a prison sentence if he caused any trouble on board. Eddie agreed to this and went to sleep ready for the task ahead of him the next day.

The next day, Eddie met with a new contact for the Germans, who asked for his story once again and also took the pages of secret writing from him. Eddie decided to take a risk at this point. He asked for some bombs that he could plant on the ship. When he was studying under Dr Akkerman, he had learned about drilling into a piece of coal and then planting a bomb inside. The bomb was then detonated when the coal was shovelled into the furnace. Eddie asked for one of these so that he could plant it on the *City of Lancaster* and sabotage the ship on the journey home. While Eddie had no intention of actually sabotaging the ship, his intention was to provide samples for the British Intelligence. When MI5 managed to intercept a radio broadcast talking about this plan the next day, there was a huge panic. They thought that Eddie was double-crossing them. Ronnie Reed was sent out to Lisbon on the next flight to arrest his charge. While Ronnie had trust in Eddie, he was worried about this. He didn't know if he would make it in time to arrest Eddie, and he didn't know if Eddie was even guilty of anything.

It took two days for the Germans to match a bomb to the coal that was used on board the ship, and thusly handed Eddie two coal bombs. Eddie told them that he would hide the coal in with the ship's coal stores that evening and then join up with them the next morning. Eddie boarded the ship and stashed his rucksack containing the bombs in his locker. He then sized up the crew to find someone who would willingly fight back.

He spotted a large Irish man and, without warning, punched him dead in the nose. The fight was on until Eddie was felled with a headbutt to his eye. The ruckus fizzled out, with Eddie and the other man both fined half a day's pay and given a public roasting.

The next morning, Eddie was tasked with taking breakfast into the captain. Once in there, he showed him the contents of his rucksack. He told the captain about how he wanted to get these bombs into British hands, and that they were safe unless heated. The captain placed them in the safe, gave Eddie his remaining possessions, shook hands, and said goodbye to Eddie Chapman.

It wasn't until that evening that Ronnie Reed arrived in Lisbon. The British Intelligence Service had already received information that Eddie had completed his mission for the Germans. When Ronnie was given this information, he was downhearted. He decided that he needed to speak to the captain, at least to ensure that none of the coal was used when the ship departed. When Ronnie arrived, however, the look of delight on the captain's face confused him. The captain could hardly contain himself when he began to tell Ronnie all about Eddie. He told Ronnie about the coal bombs and that Eddie had suggested they stage a fake explosion to increase Eddie's standing within the German organisation. Ronnie began to feel bad that he had ever doubted Eddie, especially when the captain informed him that the ship's course information being given to the Germans had been agreed upon by the captain as information they were already aware of. Ronnie instantly sent a telegram home informing his superiors that Eddie had performed his job magnificently. All they needed to do now was find a way to convince the Germans that their bombs had worked; otherwise, Eddie could be in danger. By this point, Eddie was boarding a plane to Madrid with a Norwegian passport under the name Olaf Christiansson.

When Eddie landed at Madrid airport, he was greeted by a German man who quietly asked him if he was 'Fritz.' Eddie replied with yes and recited his password to him. The man then took Eddie to the Hotel Florida, where Eddie remained for five days, dining on the best food and drinking the best wine. He was questioned again numerous times by different people, each time sticking to his story perfectly, until finally he was given some money to buy some clothes and stock up on some harder to get items such as tea and coffee.

Once his story had been told to almost everyone in Madrid, Eddie was taken by train to Bordeaux. Upon his arrival in Bordeaux, he was greeted by one of his old friends from the villa in Nantes. As they were driving to their next destination in Paris, Eddie asked him what had happened to the head German officer from when he was trained. He was told in hushed tones that he had been sent to the frontline in disgrace. Eddie was disappointed about this for several reasons. Firstly, he had seen the head officer almost as a friend while in Nantes. He had taken a shine to Eddie and regularly spoke frankly and honestly with him. Secondly, this threw up some problems regarding Eddie's safety. The head officer had been an advocate for Eddie and ensured that he was looked after properly. His being out of the picture meant that things could change for the worse. Once they were in Paris, Eddie was questioned again by multiple people. He wasn't as happy this time, demanding that he see the former head German officer. This was ignored as was Eddie's request for the money that was owed to him. Eddie was starting to feel uneasy about everything, and it took an angry protest for him to receive a small advance on the money of 20,000 francs. Even this was handed over with great reluctance. Eddie had expected to be welcomed back with open arms, after all, as for all the Germans knew, he had delivered on his mission completely. Eddie stuck to what he had learned from the British when reciting his story and managed to convince the Germans over the course of numerous retellings that he had been loyal to them. Eddie remained in Paris for ten days before he was told that he would be travelling to Berlin. Here was where the real test would lie.

The good fortune that was shining down on Eddie managed to last while he was in Berlin. He slipped up slightly while being questioned again, switching the sides of the batteries on the suitcases used for the bombing of De Havilland, but his ability at telling untruths managed to get him out of a sticky situation as he told them there were two suitcases with batteries on either side.

The day after Eddie had almost made the biggest mistake of his life, he was approached by a tall man who gave Eddie a new passport. A German passport. It was made out in the name Fritz Graumann, and in the space reserved for father it had the name Stephan Graumann. The head officer during

Eddie's time at Nantes was Dr Graumann. Eddie began to wonder if he was being taken to see him. He was told to pack his bags and be ready to leave for Norway within the hour.

What Eddie didn't know during this time was that the Germans were starting to worry about the *City of Lancaster*. The bomb hadn't gone off yet, and they were starting to become annoyed by this. They didn't suspect Eddie of double-crossing them, but they were starting to wonder if he was incompetent. The British secret services were intercepting a number of messages from German officers asking whether the ship had been blown up yet. They needed to do something quickly or Eddie was in grave danger.

The higher-ups within the British secret service were adamant that the *City of Lancaster* could not actually be blown up, so there needed to be a plan to make it seem like there had been an explosion on board. Ronnie Reed dreamed up an elaborate plan that included a fake explosion, being planted on board after the ship docked, that would create a lot of noise and smoke but not actually damage anything. This plan was vetoed by the higher-ups, though, and Ronnie had to think on his feet. Instead, he decided to rely on the use of gossip. When the *City of Lancaster* came in to dock, it was instantly besieged by a team of field security police who headed straight for the coal bunker. Here they threw pieces of coal into the dock, even adding a theatrical duck as they threw each piece. Eventually, they emerged with a piece of coal, each treating it like it was gold dust.

Afterwards, all the crew were interrogated for hours on end. As each crew member was taken one by one, rumours of Eddie's actions spread like a viral infection around the docks of Glasgow. Everyone from the owners of bars to the head of German intelligence had heard about the German spy who had tried to sabotage a British ship. Ronnie had done his job, and Eddie was not only safe, but held in the highest regard.

Upon Eddie's arrival in Norway, he was greeted by Dr Graumann. Eddie was pleased to see him, despite his own betrayal of him over the last three months. He regarded Dr Graumann as his friend. Eddie was informed that he would be allowed some time to have a holiday, but first, he would need to be interrogated one final time to collate a report to be sent to Berlin. Eddie wasn't too happy about another interrogation, but he knew it was a necessity. This time it would be Dr Graumann himself who would be carrying it out. It started the next day and lasted a full two weeks. Every single detail of everything that Eddie had done was gone over with a fine-toothed comb. It was almost like Eddie was back in England practicing his story.

Eddie was given a comfortable room in a local hotel and given 500 kroner to spend. Dr Graumann told him that he could have more money when he needed it, and that his full reward would be paid to him as soon as Berlin had cleared the report. Eddie tried to relax and enjoy himself in Norway but found it difficult. The Norwegian people were not happy at being occupied by the Germans and had taken to giving anyone who was with them the cold shoulder. Eddie enjoyed socialising and found this hard to take. He found that Norway was not going to be the same experience as France. Dr Graumann had the final version of Eddie's report typed up and boarded a plane to Berlin. This would decide whether Eddie got his reward or was 'removed' from duty. There was no warning given to Eddie that there could be a negative reaction to his activities in Britain. What he didn't know was that there were rumblings from higher-ups that they thought Eddie was lying about his activities. Fortunately, once his report was correlated with newspaper reports from England, they were convinced he was legitimate. Dr Graumann returned with good news: Eddie's reward had been cleared. He would receive 100,000 Reichsmarks for his work in England as well as an additional 10,000 for his attempt to blow up the *City of Lancaster*. This was actually less than he had been promised, but Eddie knew better than to challenge this.

There was also something else that was given to Eddie after Dr Graumann returned from Berlin. He gave Eddie a leather case that contained the Iron Cross. The highest honour that can be bestowed on a German soldier. Not only had Eddie successfully managed to hoodwink the Germans, but he had also managed to become a war hero in the process. To this day,

Eddie is the only British citizen to ever receive an Iron Cross. While in Norway, Eddie was taught how to sail. He thought that this meant his next mission would be a seafaring one. He also had to spend some time keeping his hand in with Morse code and using a wireless, although he was never trusted enough to be left alone with a wireless. Eddie was given his own camera and film and ordered to learn photography. He assumed it was just part of his next mission and so took to the job with his usual enthusiasm.

Eddie went to Dr Graumann one day and told him that he wanted to buy a boat. Dr Graumann had been acting as Eddie's banker, mainly to ensure that Eddie didn't just vanish once he had all the reward money in his possession. Eddie had only been joking so was taken aback when the doctor pulled out a pile of money for Eddie to purchase his vessel. He went down to the yard and, with the help of one of his companions, bought himself a Swedish yawl. His sailing lessons had been going well, and he was even given the chance to sail alone, although in typical Eddie Chapman fashion he needed to be towed back to the harbour after losing his sails. This act of foolish bravery just enhanced his standing with the Germans—they admired his bravery, even if it was tinged with foolishness.

Chapter 7: From Norway To London

Eddie had taken to life in Norway like a duck to water. The only thing he was missing was the social aspect that he loved so much. He enjoyed the company of his German handlers, but he knew that they were there to keep an eye on him as well as be his friend. Eddie wanted some more organic friendship, and he also wanted the company of a woman. It was late April when he finally got his wish. Eddie met Dagmar Lahlum in the Ritz in Oslo. She thought he was a German officer so gave him the usual cold shoulder but eventually warmed to Eddie as his natural charm and charisma wore her down. Dagmar wasn't just any Norwegian girl, though. That she was drinking in a known German officers' bar should have thrown up a red flag to Eddie, but he wasn't thinking straight. He just saw a beautiful woman, and he wanted to get to know her better.

It was a strange relationship, as both sides had secrets

they couldn't tell the other. Eddie couldn't tell Dagmar that he was really a British spy working as a double agent, and Dagmar couldn't tell Eddie that she was working for the resistance in secret. They were both working on the same side but didn't know it. Perhaps it was fate that brought them together. Whatever it was led them to realise over time that they were kindred spirits. Much like the arrangement back in Britain, Eddie was moved into a safe house, and he moved Dagmar in with him. The house had once belonged to some Norwegian Jews, but they had been removed from the house and executed. It was during this time that Eddie would take up the habit of taking photographs of the various people in the house. He cultivated this habit so that it wouldn't appear strange or out of the ordinary if he did so when people of interest entered the household.

During May, Eddie was taken to Berlin for the day. Once he was there he was interviewed about the De Havilland sabotage as well as other potential targets. The SS officer who was conducting the interview was drunk the whole way through, and Eddie never knew if this was a way to try and make him drop his guard or just a lack of professionalism. Once the interview was over, Eddie returned to Norway with some new knowledge. The Germans were planning to send him back to England, potentially to carry out another sabotage. He needed to get some information together to pass on to the British, and quickly. Although Eddie didn't have anything written down, he had been using his remarkable memory for places and faces to make note of anything that he thought might be of use. Names and descriptions of people he saw, areas that would be possible targets for strategic bombing, and general information about the German occupation of Norway. It was around this time that Eddie revealed to Dagmar that he was a British spy. The relief on her face was almost as much of a shock to Eddie as when she told him that she was a member of the resistance.

Once Eddie and Dagmar were both aware of who the other actually was, they began to work together like a well-oiled machine. She found out information for him as well as acting as a model for when he wanted to take photographs of potentially important places. It looked a lot less suspicious if a man was taking pictures of his girlfriend posing than if a man was just taking a picture of a military installation. When Eddie turned twenty-nine, he had a birthday party. Dagmar spent the evening taking photographs of everyone who turned up. Eddie hid the film, ready to be removed at a moment's notice. The partnership of the two spies was a fruitful relationship and allowed Eddie to collect a lot more information than he would have operating alone.

On the 10th of July 1943, Dagmar entered a shop while Eddie waited outside. When she emerged, she was excited and told Eddie the good news. The Allies had invaded Sicily. As the news wouldn't have been revealed in any German-occupied territories due to strict propaganda laws, she must have found it out from one of her resistance compatriots.

By the end of the summer, Eddie was called into Dr Graumann's office. Here he was shown a new contract for him to sign. The new contract was for 'new sabotage work'. Eddie had a problem with this new contract for two reasons. Firstly, he felt that he deserved to know exactly what he was signing up for. It would be easy for the Germans to renege on the deal if the contract was generic. Secondly, he felt that he was okay financially, so unless the reward was significant, he had no reason to risk his life. Dr Graumann was furious at Eddie's insolence, but Eddie was resolute in his refusal. Eddie was in no rush to sign—he knew that they needed him more than he needed them. Not only that, but he could use it as an excuse to spend more time with Dagbar.

It took a week before Dr Graumann relented and flew to Berlin to try and organise something more concrete for Eddie. This came after a week of flipping between trying to strongarm Eddie into signing the contract and using the various handlers to try and talk Eddie round. None of it worked, so a trip to Berlin was his last resort. When he returned, he was in much better spirits and informed Eddie that there was a new job on the table for him. He was being tasked with finding out why the German U-Boats were no longer effective. The Germans weren't aware that their enigma code had been cracked by Bletchley Park. Because of this, they were under the assumption that the British had some new underwater tracking device. They didn't realise that the British were privy to the movements of their submarines just from decoding messages. Eddie was given a range of information that the Germans already knew, or thought they knew, about the submarine detection system, and was told he would be trained in how to recognise the device and potentially steal one. For this, Eddie was to be paid 600,000 Reichsmarks, which was an amount significantly greater than what he had been paid for his original mission.

While all of this was going on, the Luftwaffe had plans for Eddie to carry out another job. Just as the German submarines had been the targets of surprise attacks, their planes had been suffering the same. The few Allied planes that they had managed to shoot down were equipped with a device that they didn't recognise. None of the planes had a device in good enough condition for them to get it working. Eddie was to be tasked with finding a working one and bringing it to them.

While the two arms of the German secret service were busy fighting over who got Eddie first, Eddie was making himself busy leading seminars on espionage and even teaching students how to use the wireless to send messages. Eddie's fake attack on the De Havilland factory had made him the most experienced and successful spy that they had. This meant that he was de facto the best person to teach the next generation of spies how to carry out their mission. Unfortunately for Eddie, his students were willing, but they were not able. The level of intellect to be a successful spy was far greater than the students possessed.

A decision was arrived at regarding Eddie's mission. He would carry out the naval mission as his main target, with the plane radar mission being a secondary objective. In return for the naval mission taking precedence, the German Navy would pay for the mission. This was an acceptable resolution for all parties and plans for Eddie to return to England were set in motion. Eddie knew that Dagmar could be in danger if he wasn't there to look after her. He also knew that he would be unable to take her with him. So, before he left, he made arrangements with Dr Graumann that Dagmar be given somewhere to live as well as a monthly allowance to allow her to live comfortably. Dr Graumann agreed to this, knowing that Dagmar's safety was paramount to maintaining Eddie's loyalty. In typical Eddie Chapman fashion, he now had two women being looked after by two warring factions. Before Eddie left, he set his new signal to be added to the front of his wireless messages, replacing 'FFFFF'. He would now start all his messages with 'DAGMAR' as a sign of respect as well as reminding his German taskmasters exactly who they needed to keep safe to keep his loyalty.

While Eddie was getting ready to make his trip to England, three men were spotted in Iceland behaving in a suspicious manner. After being picked up by the British secret services, they were taken to London. It was here that they admitted they had been trained in the art of espionage in Germany by a man with a high-pitched voice and in bad German. As more details became clear, they started to wonder if this man was Eddie. They showed the men a picture of Eddie, and it confirmed their suspicions. Eddie was alive and still active. They didn't know when and if he was coming back, but that he was still alive meant that he hadn't been discovered as a double agent.

All of this was going on while Eddie was waiting to make the trip to England. Every time he seemed about to make the move across the channel, something else cropped up to delay his trip. By early June 1944, he had been called to make the trip twice and had it cancelled each time. He was starting to feel that he would be spending the rest of the war with the Germans.

That all changed on the 27th of June. Eddie was told that he would be flying from Holland. His mission had been added to again. His new mission was to inform the Germans of how effective their new V1 flying bombs had been. He now had three missions to attend to while in England. Find the submarine tracking system, get hold of a working radar from one of their planes, and report on the accuracy of the flying bombs. Eddie was suddenly tasked with carrying out three missions vital to the German war effort. This spoke volumes of the reverence that Eddie was held in by the Germans. They truly believed that he was fully loyal and highly skilled. The British couldn't have a better agent in place than Eddie Chapman. Before Eddie left, he was given the best equipment that the Germans had available. Two cameras, a new wireless radio, a collection of poisons, a revolver, and £6,000.

Chapter 8: End Of The War And Beyond

Eddie informed the British officers exactly what his new task would be, and it was in this that the first real headache was encountered. He had to pass on a camera and some of the money to another agent. The British were well aware of this agent, as they had also managed to turn him double agent. This meant that the handover of the camera and money would require the fabrication of two sets of false stories so as to maintain the safety of both agents. The British didn't want to have their two double agents forming any kind of link to each other, but to keep up the charade, they knew that it would be unavoidable. Despite this problem, the British were extremely excited by the return of Eddie and especially the information that he had provided them. The depth of his mission meant that there would be numerous chances to deceive the Germans and stunt their chances of clawing back any ground regarding the war.

Although the British thought Chapman perfectly loyal, they were troubled by his introduction of Dagmar to operations. She was an unknown quantity, and they didn't know whether it was a matter of time before their whole double agent program was blown out of the water. It was decided that this mission would be the last that Eddie would undertake. He was too much of a loose cannon, and they didn't know if he would end up bringing them more trouble than he was worth. Eddie wasn't informed of this choice just yet, and on the 30th of June, he sent his arrival message to the Germans: *'HARD LANDING BUT ALL OK. FINDING BETTER PLACE. COMING AGAIN THURSDAY. DAGMAR.'*

The V1 flying bombs had been hitting London since the 13th of June. They tended to fall short of the centre of London, and this led to British intelligence devising a plan to ensure that it stayed this way. They would tell Eddie to pass on the information that the bombs were being overshot. This would cause them to divert their aim even further south and into the countryside rather than the densely populated area of central London. It took some persuading for the government to agree to the plan, as perversely they believed that the people of London were used to the bombings and diverting the bombs to less populated areas of the country that were unscathed would lower morale. Fortunately, reason won the day, and the plan was agreed to. On the 1st of July, Eddie sent his first report to the Germans detailing the level of accuracy of their bombing campaign. For a full month, Eddie sent faulty intelligence to the Germans, with advanced physicists helping to ensure that the location given was consistent with the time it should have taken to reach that point. It was meticulously planned because it was such an important mission. If the Germans rumbled that they were being fed the wrong information, then not only would it cause them to lose Eddie as a viable double agent, but it would also cause them to correct their aim and begin hitting the capital with much more force.

While the German bombs did continue to hit England and indeed kill a significant number of people, they were diverted to more sparsely populated areas, which not only limited the damage but also reduced the number of civilians killed. This continued until the 25th of July, when the plan was suspended for two reasons. Firstly, British newspapers had begun to print detailed maps of the areas that were damaged by the bombs. If this didn't tally up with the information that Eddie was passing onto the Germans, then it would most certainly rumble him. As well as this, the Americans had developed their radar capabilities to the point where they could shoot down the majority of the V1 bombs while they were still in flight.

Within a month, the V1 threat had been nullified and Eddie was starting to become idle again. The British were starting to worry. They knew that if Eddie became bored, there was a chance he would start to engage in criminal activity again. There was also the problem that he was still wanted by the police. MI5 decided to solve this problem by issuing a pardon for Eddie. All his pre-war convictions were expunged, although they didn't tell Eddie this—they wanted to keep him in check after all. They needed something to occupy Eddie's interest, and the Germans' worry about the U-boats seemed like the perfect plan.

It was decided that Eddie would get in touch with the Germans and inform them that he had managed to find a factory in the north of England where a submarine detection device was being manufactured. He would then send them a document via the wireless and send photographs through Lisbon. The documents and photographs were to amplify the abilities of the British 'hedgehogs' that were attached to their ships. These devices were explosives that activated on impact with a submarine. Eddie was to send them documents saying that the hedgehogs had proximity fuses that could trigger them if a U-boat was within a certain distance as well as triggering other depth charges. The depth charges were to have a range of up to 15 metres, which meant that the U-boats would have to keep their distance even more. It was ingenious.

As the Germans were already afraid of the British anti-submarine measures, to amplify this fear could help the war effort. The fear of the hedgehogs would lead to the U-boats being afraid to drop to deeper levels and leave them exposed when they were closer to the surface. The British Intelligence had managed to create a level of fear and worry in the Germans without developing any new technology at all. The combination of Bletchley Park and Eddie Chapman meant that their ships were safer than ever.

The details were all worked out, but as the plan was formed, wheels were put in motion that started the end for Eddie Chapman as a wartime spy. Ronnie Reed was moved to France to act as head of intelligence for the American forces. Eddie didn't just see Ronnie as his boss, he saw Ronnie as a friend, and his moving was not good for his morale. In addition to this, his replacement, Michael Ryde, clashed with Eddie from the start. He was a stickler for the rules, and this didn't sit well with Eddie's more fast and loose approach. Michael Ryde had advanced to his position through nepotism—his father-in-law was a man with great political power within MI5. After his initial clashes with Eddie, he decided that it was best to get rid of Eddie as soon as possible. He just needed to wait for the right moment.

Eddie liked to go drinking on his off days, and Ryde bristled at this. He liked a drink, himself; he just didn't like drinking with Eddie. He found him tiresome and a bore. He started to limit the money that Eddie had access to. It was a good plan as this led to Eddie becoming bored with life as a secret agent. All it was at the moment was sending messages by wireless. This wasn't to his tastes at all.

Ryde was a high functioning alcoholic who by the time he died had managed to end two marriages. He was an abrasive man, especially when confronted with people he felt were beneath him. Eddie was definitely someone that Ryde felt was beneath him. He made it his mission to discredit Eddie as much as possible. Ryde knew that this wouldn't be achieved instantly, but if he threw enough mud, some of it would stick. As soon as there was enough mud there, he would strike.

When Ryde wrote a report saying that the Agent Zigzag case should be closed at the earliest possible moment, his superiors overruled him and showed their own support for Eddie by insisting that it should be closed at the latest possible moment. They were aware that Eddie was becoming restless, and they knew that if he wasn't found something to do soon, there was a good chance he could go rogue.

MI5 managed to procure photographs of the 'hedgehog' that didn't give away any actual information, and Eddie told the Germans that he would use a seaman friend of his to smuggle the photo to them in Lisbon. He told them that he would convince the man he was smuggling drugs in order not to arouse any espionage-based suspicions, but in reality, it was just MI5 delivering the photo to the Germans. Once this was delivered, the Germans became incredibly excited and asked for more information about the proximity fuses.

It is at this point in the story where Agent Zigzag meets

James Bond, literally! To confuse the Germans, a young man working in naval intelligence, by the name of Ian Fleming, was enlisted to help create a believable backstory for the proximity fuse. It was from this plan that a scientist by the name of Fleming was invented to be the subject of a letter explaining some of the more intricate details about the fuse that Eddie found. He then sent the contents of this letter to the Germans over wireless to lead them on a wild goose chase. The Germans would be wasting their time trying to find a solution to a problem that didn't exist. It was a perfect plan by the British: it would allow Eddie to remain undetected while at the same time both wasting German resources and stopping them from discovering that the Enigma code had been cracked.

Could it be possible that some of the adventures that James Bond went on were carried out by Eddie Chapman? It's no secret that Ian Fleming used his experiences during the war to craft his stories and ensure that they had an element of realism. While it has never been confirmed, there is definitely a chance that Eddie Chapman was one influence on one of the most famous fictional spies of all time.

Despite all his sterling work, Eddie was being undermined constantly by Ryde. He consistently expressed doubts as to whether the photographs would manage to make their way to the Germans and pointed to a cancelled meeting with a fellow double agent to show the Germans were losing trust in Eddie as well as a politician letting it slip about where the V1 rockets were really landing, all to show that Eddie was not the valuable commodity they thought. All the while that this was going on, Eddie had started to fall back into his old ways. He had discovered that the local dog racing was being fixed; his old criminal gang were doping dogs in the races. This led to Eddie often being able to predict the winner and led to a betting scam from which he made a big profit that he then split with his tipster. It all came to a head when Eddie turned up late to send a message to the Germans because he had been at the dog track.

The decision was made that Eddie would be cut loose as soon as possible. The original members of the team advocated for Eddie to be financially rewarded as well as being given help to set up a business, but Ryde consistently undermined this proposition with calculated attacks on Eddie's reliability. Not that these attacks were unwarranted—Eddie had been slowly descending into his old life. He had begun hanging out at all the old criminal haunts he had previously and was slowly making Ryde's efforts easier. Fortunately for Eddie though, every time it appeared that Ryde could get the Zigzag case closed, the Germans wanted more information from Eddie. He consistently showed his worth, and that ensured that the higher-ups in the British secret services wanted Eddie around for as long as possible.

The biggest victory that Eddie had in his personal war with Ryde was when the Germans sent him the serial numbers of all the devices that they had found from Allied planes. This allowed the British to know exactly what technology the Germans had of theirs and to plan accordingly. Ryde was both pleased and annoyed at the same time. He had to find a way to remove Eddie, preferably without rewarding him financially at the same time. Ryde didn't have to wait long—as is typical of Eddie, his mouth did Ryde's job for him.

Eddie began to discuss money with Ryde, who felt that Eddie had been financially remunerated enough already. Eddie disagreed with this, and the two men argued. Eddie ended up sending a message to the Germans telling them that he needed more money. Ryde was all for this development, as he knew the Germans had a habit of sending fake money to their agents. If they sent Eddie fake money, he knew, it would destroy Eddie's faith in them and give him a shot to close the case. Before this could happen, though, Eddie made his first of two fatal errors. He admitted to Ryde while talking about Dr Graumann that he knew that he was embezzling some of Eddie's money for himself. This admittance of financial collusion between the two men led Ryde to believe that Eddie was in league with Dr Graumann and had, in fact, informed him that he was a British double agent. While this wasn't the case, the suspicion was enough for Ryde to begin ramping up his campaign to have Eddie removed from his position. Ryde got his moment in late October.

An MI5 agent called round to Eddie's residence

unannounced—possibly sent by Ryde—looking for information. When he got there, he was shocked to see several of the criminal underworld in the flat, Eddie's old cohorts, as well as the newly released from prison Jimmy Hunt. Eddie was nowhere to be seen, and as the agent looked around the room, Jimmy rose from his seat and with a knowing smile said, 'I suppose you've come to take Eddie away on another job.' The agent made his excuses and reported back to Ryde.

With his suspicions about Dr Graumann combined with the evidence that Eddie had told Jimmy Hunt of his activities, Ryde had what he needed. These two bits of trouble on top of the situation with Dagmar meant that Ryde felt Eddie's position was tenuous. He presented his evidence to the higher-ups within MI5, and they agreed completely. Eddie was made to sign the Official Secrets Act and was informed that if he told people what he had done during the war he would be prosecuted and imprisoned. Once he had signed this, he was thrown out of his flat. Ryde lectured him about how it was his own lack of responsibility that had caused the problem, and if he had behaved in a proper manner, it would never have come to this. Eddie was allowed to keep any money that was left over from what the Germans had given him, but the British didn't pay him anything. Ryde had finally managed to make enough mud stick to Eddie—his long-term plan had finally come to fruition.

Ryde had spent his entire time in his job posting trying to

remove Eddie Chapman, and he had finally managed it. Not only was he pleased that Eddie was no longer part of MI5, he was also pleased with himself for managing it. Perhaps if Ronnie Reed had remained in position until the end of the war things may have gone differently for Eddie, but that is something we will never know.

While Eddie's misdeeds near the end were undoubtedly his own fault, he was also well within his rights to feel slightly hard done by. He had risked his life numerous times, extorted money from the German war effort, given the Germans false information on numerous occasions and provided incredibly valuable information to the Secret Service Bureau. For his efforts, he was thrown onto the streets with a lecture and a threat of imprisonment. Eddie didn't see it that way, though. He felt rewarded by both sides that he had worked for. The Germans had paid him handsomely and even rewarded him with a medal, and the British had expunged him of the crimes he had committed before the war. As well as this, he was free to make the most of the burgeoning wartime black market. War had made it easy for men like Eddie to make money, and now he didn't have the secret services breathing down his neck, Eddie intended to make up for lost time.

Before Eddie made the move back into crime, though, he had a mission that was much closer to his heart to attend to. When Eddie jumped out of a closed window in Jersey, he had been eating trifle with a young lady named Betty Farmer. Now

Eddie was free, he intended to find her again. Freda may have given him a daughter, Dagmar may have been a kindred spirit, but Betty was whom he really loved. He used some of the money he had made from the Germans to hire a private investigator as well as get in touch with his two minders from his first stay in Britain as a spy. They managed to trace Betty to a hotel on the Isle of Man in 1943, but after that, the trail went cold. It was much harder to find people in the 1940s, and especially without a photo. Eddie convened with the men to try and describe Betty to them.

They met up at the Berkeley Hotel in Knightsbridge. While the men sat eating lunch, he pointed to a young lady who was sat with her back to them. 'From behind,' he told them 'she looks exactly the same as Betty.' As the men turned around to look at her, by chance she turned around as well. Eddie was shocked to see that it was Betty. He made his way over to her side, where she was equally shocked to see him. They renewed their acquaintances over time, and not long after they got married. In 1954, they had a daughter together, making Eddie a father again. Despite Eddie's still being a man who liked the company of ladies, Betty always forgave him, and their marriage lasted until Eddie's death.

Once Eddie had found Betty, he threw himself into his criminal work with gusto. Eddie bought his way into a gold smuggling gang led by a crooked nightclub owner named Billy Hill. They tried to smuggle cigarettes and even kidnap a sultan, but it went wrong when they got into a brawl at the docks. Coming back to England in the 1950s, Billy's gang robbed a post office van, making away with £250,000 which is worth about £2,600,000 today. By the 1960s, Eddie and Betty had moved to Africa to carry out a building contract, but it wasn't long before there were allegations of corruption. Eddie wasn't worried about these allegations—he'd already made the trip home before they managed to implicate him in anything.

Although Eddie was astute at getting himself out of trouble on the occasions that he was caught for various crimes, he used his contacts to get himself out of trouble. In 1948, he was arrested for using fake money. He managed to avoid jail after a character reference from a senior officer at the war office. The officer was unnamed, but it is thought that it was Eddie's old friend Ronnie Reed. In 1974, after being arrested for smashing a glass over another man's head during a bar fight, he informed the court that his wartime training meant that he had no need to use a glass in a fight. The jury believed him, and he was acquitted of all charges. Eddie knew that as long as he didn't get caught doing anything too bad, his wartime service would help him to remain out of jail.

The Hill Gang slowly dispersed over time, but Eddie still maintained an interest in petty crime to supplement his lifestyle. He could never get a proper job. He just knew that he didn't have the dedication for it. Crime paid well, and Eddie was good enough not to get caught. He continued associating with criminals for as long as he could.

In the 1950s, Eddie turned his hand at trying to make some legitimate money. He wrote a book based on his exploits during the war. Just like those of other wartime spies and spymasters, Eddie's book was blocked. He attempted to write a version of his story that had removed all the parts that strayed into what was covered by the Official Secrets Act. He did manage to get this printed in a French newspaper, but when he approached the *News of the World*, MI5 got wind of it. This led to a complete edition of the paper being pulped and Eddie being fined £50.

In 1954, Eddie managed to get a version of his story released. *The Eddie Chapman* story told of his time in Germany, but it didn't cover any of his time with MI5. The newspapers went in for the kill upon its release. They decried Eddie as a traitor to his country. The Official Secrets Act forbade Eddie from making any kind of rebuttal to these claims, so he had to suffer the indignity of this all the time with the knowledge that he had served his country. In 1957, he managed to satisfy his literary itch by ghostwriting the autobiography of Eric Pleasants, who according to Eddie had been imprisoned with him in Jersey or France. While there is no evidence or records to show that the two men had served time together, there is no reason to doubt the claims either, except perhaps that each man was using the other to garner financial reward.

It took until 1966 for Eddie to set the record straight with the release of *The Real Eddie Chapman Story*, which covered his time with MI5 while still being careful not to give away too much information. It acted as a rebuttal to the newspapers that had accused him of being a traitor as well as providing Eddie and his family with a legitimate income. It ended up being made into a movie called *Triple Cross*, which Eddie was not too fond of. He felt that it wasn't true to the source material and didn't give him the fame and adulation that he felt he was due. This was in part because Eddie was banned from entering France to supervise the filming of the movie, as he was still wanted for the plot to kidnap the sultan.

This was the one thing that Eddie truly regretted about his wartime activities. He was never fully appreciated for what he did, and this weighed heavy on him at times over the years. Eddie also felt remorse for some of the people who had suffered in his stead. Anthony Faramus and Dagmar Lahlum were the two main ones. Once the war ended, Eddie was delighted to find out that Anthony was alive and well. He met up with him once in a meeting organised by a journalist. The two men spoke, and Anthony admitted that he was tempted once or twice to give up Eddie in order to procure his own freedom but decided against it because he didn't want to do anything to help the people who were hurting him so much. Eddie felt bad for everything that Anthony had gone through, even feeling as though it was partly his fault. The two men spent the evening in the pub getting drunk and talking about old times. In a slice of irony, Anthony ended up working as an actor in Hollywood and played a prisoner in Colditz.

Dagmar ended up being fined and given a six-month suspended sentence in 1947 for consorting with a German officer. While the people in her village spent their time gossiping behind her back, Dagmar never betrayed Eddie— this despite his breaking his promise to come back for her. Eddie and Dagmar never saw each other again. It wasn't until she died, when a letter was found by her niece, that her true nature during the war was revealed. In an interview in 1994, Eddie claimed that he would have liked to have seen her again, but due to it contravening the Official Secrets Act, MI5 made sure that it was never screened. Perhaps if it had been screened, the two could have met up before their deaths in the late 1990s. Dagmar Lahlum never married and never had children, possibly due to the stigma that was attached to her after the war, but she was loyal to the man she viewed as the love of her life.

Freda and Diane didn't see much of Eddie after the war had ended. Freda was never one for standing still, and she got a job and even married twice after realising that Eddie was never going to come back into her life. While MI5 reneged on the agreement to pay her the moment that Eddie was released from their employ, she did still benefit from the savings account that had been set up in Eddie's name during his first mission. She used this to ensure that Diane never went without while growing up. Eddie may not have been there as much as he should, but in a roundabout way, he still provided for his daughter and ex-fiancée. Freda may well have been let down by Eddie, but she never let it stop her from living her life.

Eddie had managed to become the honorary crime correspondent for *The Sunday Telegraph*, where his advice consisted of telling people to steer clear of people like him. He never admitted shame for his life of crime, even saying in one interview that he thought he was an honest villain. This came through with the way he carried himself throughout his life.

The money that Eddie had accumulated throughout his life allowed him to purchase a castle in Ireland as well as setting up a health farm in Hertfordshire. This meant that Eddie finally had legitimate income. While the initial investment may have come from illicit means, the health farm meant that Eddie and Betty never had to worry about Eddie drifting into the criminal underworld again.

In 1974, Eddie bumped into someone he never thought he would see again: one of the men who had trained him to shoot during his initial training by the Germans, Leo Kreusch. He was pleased to see Eddie, and the two men reminisced about old times. It was here that Leo told Eddie that Dr Graumann had been a pseudonym. The man's real name was Stephan

Von Gröning. Before the war, he had been a German aristocrat but after the war had fallen on hard times. Eddie had always seen Von Gröning as a friend and not his superior, and he expressed to Leo that he would like to write him a letter. Leo told Eddie Von Gröning's address in Bremen and Eddie sent him a letter.

Von Gröning had been wealthy before the war started, although he had begun to go through money faster than he could make it. His own embezzling of the money Eddie had been given meant that he had been able to build up a significant amount of money again. He used this money to purchase valuable commodities. He had a suspicion that Germany was going to lose the war and that could lead to a crash in the value of their currency. He knew that paintings, gold, and other valuable items would maintain their value, so this was where he spent his money. Unfortunately for Von Gröning, a bomb hit his home where all his items were stored. He ended the war as he had started it, on the brink of financial ruin. After the war, he was arrested by American forces and kept in a prison near Bremen, he was never tried for war crimes and eventually found a job in a museum.

The two men sparked up conversation through letters as though no time had passed in the intervening years. Eddie invited Von Gröning to his daughter's wedding in 1979, and he happily attended. Betty was shocked at how close the two men were considering what had gone on between them, but she could never understand that Eddie had felt an affinity for Von Gröning. He'd never been truly a Nazi, even going as far to decry what Hitler was carrying out as barbaric. He was loyal to his country even if he wasn't happy at the methods they were using. Eddie and Von Gröning spoke all night about the old times. The final link to Eddie's past life coming back to meet him and giving him some form of closure and appreciation.

On the 11th of December 1997, Eddie Chapman suffered a fatal heart failure. He was 83 and survived by his wife Betty and his daughters Diane and Suzanne. It was a death that wasn't felt in the public eye too much. This is an unfair reflection on the impact that Eddie Chapman had on the war. His efforts ensured that the Germans didn't gain more of a foothold and hastened the end of the war. While it is likely that the Allies would have still won the war without Eddie's help, it is also likely that the war could have carried on for longer, causing the death of many thousands more people. Agent Zigzag was the perfect moniker for Eddie Chapman. He tap-danced along the fine line between good and bad, certainly during the war, where to he played his German spymasters perfectly. Eddie never stopped zigging and zagging throughout his life. This was partly due to his propensity for getting bored. He said to Betty on that fateful day in the hotel in Jersey: *'I shall go, but I shall always come back.'*

This phrase is the most pertinent description of Eddie

there is. Eddie may have zigged away from Betty at times, but he always zagged back. He retreated from his country but always returned at the first opportunity. Then, his life of crime received the same treatment.

In the end, Agent Zigzag wasn't a name made up for Eddie, it was a name he was born into.

About Ethan Quinn

Ethan Quinn lives in the beautifully rural county of Herefordshire with his wife and child. In his spare time, he enjoys many different activities, such as walking, bouldering, and playing the traditional English sport of cricket.

Ethan has always been fascinated with people and the stories that they can tell. He believes that people are the most creative, unique, and surprising things on this planet, and some are more extraordinary than others. He strives to find out what drives these exceptional human beings to become what they are and do what they do, which is not always for good!

Ethan has a background in writing, and in 2017 he decided to follow his passion to write in the True Crime Espionage area about the incredible humans that become spies.

When writing he always tries to concentrate on the truth, and highlights what makes these people truly remarkable. This is done with complete honesty and attempting to understand their point of view because as mentioned earlier, these unique individuals didn't always stay within the law.

For more information about the author and his latest releases please visit Ethan Quinn's website:

WWW.ETHANQUINNBOOKS.COM

More Books by Ethan Quinn

Many terms were bestowed upon the mysterious Fritz Duquesne throughout his colourful life, but perhaps the most fitting ever attributed to him was: **"The most dangerous prisoner to have ever lived."**

Fritz Duquesne was a Boer War warrior-turned-spy who vowed revenge against the nation which took from him those he held dear. This lead to his own enrolment in the military of whichever side fought opposite the British forces.

Through complex prison escapes, destructive acts of sabotage, and heroic feats which are even too farfetched for fiction, Fritz Duquesne exacted revenge in the most daring, unbelievable, and all-round theatrical manner possible.

Fritz assumed many different identities and he ultimately became responsible for the largest espionage ring ever uncovered in the United States.

Free Espionage Audiobook

If you are interested in listening to the unbelievable story of Eddie Chapman, then please follow the link to download a **FREE** copy of Iron Spy

WWW.ETHANQUINNBOOKS.COM/FREE-AUDIOBOOK

"Another true tale of little known 'derring - do' by Ethan. A very insightful read of the life of an oft flawed character who demonstrated steely heroism during the Second World War - masterful!" **K.E. Fellows**

"The amazing story of Eddie Chapman until now has been a long lost secret within 20th century wartime history. A great piece of writing from Ethan Quinn to bring this important piece of history to life." **J Thomas**

"...Here's another brilliant double agent story that'll have you hooked from beginning to end. A must read!" **H. Davies**

"Another fantastic biography from Ethan Quinn. This real life story of Eddie Chapman will have you gripped and not wanting to put it down. You won't believe this really happened." **G. Probert**

WWW.ETHANQUINNBOOKS.COM/FREE-AUDIOBOOK

Made in the USA
Monee, IL
13 July 2020